HEAD TO TOE

kids' knit accessories

KATYA FRANKEL

Cooperative Press

CLEVELAND, OHIO

HEAD TO TOE

Library of Congress Control Number: 2013953714
ISBN 13: 978-1-937513-34-4
First Edition
Published by Cooperative Press
www.cooperativepress.com

Knitter' Symbols fonts used courtesy Knitter's Magazine—
Copyright © 1998 XRX, Inc.

Liebe Erika font by LiebeDesigns

Models: Anthony, Bridget, Joseph, Luke, Sophie, and Timothy

Every effort has been made to ensure that all the information in
this book is accurate at the time of publication. Cooperative Press
neither endorses nor guarantees the content of external links
referenced in this book. All business names, trademarks and product
names used within the text are the property of their respective
owners. If you have questions or comments about this book, or
need information about licensing, custom editions, special sales, or
academic/corporate purchases, please contact Cooperative Press:
info@cooperativepress.com or 13000 Athens Ave C288, Lakewood,
OH 44107 USA

FOR COOPERATIVE PRESS
Senior Editor: Shannon Okey
Art Director/Assistant Editor: Elizabeth Green Musselman
Technical Editor: Joeli Caparco

To Mum and Dad

TABLE OF CONTENTS

HEAD THINGS

NECK THINGS

HAND THINGS

FOOT THINGS

INTRODUCTION

Autumn comes all at once in England. One day, mid-September, you just happen to notice that the trees have started turning, and the nip in the air reflexively makes you stretch towards the hat bin in the hallway. To me, autumn always means both making and wearing accessories.

And knitting accessories for children is the ultimate example of instant gratification: those pieces are quick to make and always well received.

Working on this book, I set out to include a variety of projects for knitters that enjoy textural, cable, or colorwork accessories so you can dress your children from head to toe.

Many of the patterns in this book are named for sites and features in stunning Northumberland National and Country Parks, near where I live.

I hope you enjoy the book!

THINGS TO KNOW

The patterns in this book come complete with a list of finished measurements and, if appropriate, a list of "to fit" measurements to help you choose the correct size. Because all children grow at different rates there is simply no universally accepted size/age system when it comes to accessories, and working from actual measurements is the only way to get the correct fit.

The size and ease tables provided on the next page will help you choose the right size to make.

Yarn Substitution

A lot of thought went into finding the right yarn for each design, so it is important to choose any substitutions carefully. There are a number of things to keep in mind when substituting yarns. Most yarn labels include a suggested gauge and needle size, which can be a good starting point for selecting an alternative. But besides matching yarn weight and gauge, you should also consider the yarn's fiber content, as well as the knitted fabric's hand and drape. Other things to consider are care, washing instructions, and fiber softness. The yarns you would use for hats and scarves should preferably be soft to touch; sock and glove yarn should be more durable in order to withstand wear.

Swatching

Circular knitting often produces a different gauge than flat knitting does. For items knit in the round, your swatch should be made in the round, too.

There are two ways to go about swatching in the round. The most obvious one is to cast on a number of stitches that is approximately double the number given in your gauge, join and work in the round as you would for any circular piece. This works great for larger gauge yarns. For finer ones, however, making a circular swatch of 40-odd stitches is a long affair.

Working a flat swatch in the round is a great time saver. Swatches done this way are worked on double-pointed needles and on the right side of your piece only. Although the edge stitches in this swatch might ruffle, it produces the same result as a knit-in-the-round piece does, and takes very little time to finish.

To make a flat swatch "in the round," cast on at least 4 inches' worth of stitches and work the first row. At the end of the row, slip the stitches to the opposite end of your double-pointed needle and bring the yarn loosely across the back, forming a giant float across the wrong side of your swatch. Keep on working from right to left, knitting on the right side (public-facing side) only. You will have one loop of yarn along the back of your swatch for every right side row.

After making a swatch, measure and take note of your stitch and row gauges. Wash and block your swatch and measure it again. All gauges given in this book reflect what you would get after washing and blocking your swatch, not before. Always check that you get the correct gauge with whichever needles you use. Both stitch and row gauge can change significantly after a wash. Generally a simple soak and a pat-it-flat to get your stitches relaxed is enough. But if you suspect that your knitted fabric will grow, make a larger swatch and hang it to dry with some pegs (clothespins) attached at the bottom to simulate the garment weight (in proportion). Bear in mind that scarves are likely to stretch under their own weight, while mittens aren't. These "drape swatches" are essential for measuring gauge accurately on non-wool yarns in particular.

Sizing and Ease

Hat and cowl sizes are based on children's head circumference, and to fit comfortably they should be made smaller than the actual head circumference.

Sock and glove sizes are based on foot and hand circumference respectively, and should be made the same size or a little wider than that measurement. Socks should have a little wiggle room at the toe and glove fingers should be worked to the end of the fingertips before working decreases. Socks worked in a thicker yarn should have more positive ease added to them, taking into account bulkier fabric.

Tips and Techniques

Any special techniques that are unique to each pattern are listed in the pattern instructions, but here are some tips on finishing touches that you might find helpful.

WORK EACH STITCH AS IT PRESENTS ITSELF

When a pattern tells you to "work each stitch as it presents itself," this means that as you are about to work the next stitch on the left-hand needle, examine the stitch in the row/round below. If a purl bump is facing you, work that stitch as a purl. If the tell-tale V of a knit stitch is facing you, work that stitch as a knit.

STRETCHY BIND OFF

Stretchy bind offs on cowls and sock cuffs that were worked from the toe up are essential. One way to add stretch to a bind off is to work the stitches you're casting off twice. Work 2 stitches as they present themselves, *slip them back onto left-hand needle and work an ssk or a p2tog, depending on the 2nd stitch on the left-hand needle. Work next stitch as it presents itself. Repeat from * until all stitches have been worked.

Ease table

Garment	Hats and cowls	Socks & gloves – fine yarn	Socks & gloves – Aran weight or thicker
Ease to be added to body measurement	2–3" / 5–7.5cm negative ease	0–½" / 0–1.5cm positive ease	½–1" / 1.5–2.5cm positive ease

Glove and mitten size table

Age	1–3	3–5	5–8	8–12	12+
Hand circumference	4½" / 11.5cm	5–5½" / 13–14cm	6–6½" / 15–16.5cm	7" / 18cm	7½" / 19cm

Sock size table

Age	1–2	3–4	5–7	8–10	11+
Foot circumference	5½" / 14cm	6" / 15.5cm	6½" / 16.5cm	7" / 17.5cm	7½" / 19cm

Foot length based on shoe size

US size	UK size	EU size	Foot length in inches	Foot length in cm
7	6	23	5½	14
8	7	24	5¾	14.5
9	8	25.5	6¼	16
10	9	27	6½	16.5
11	10	28	6¾	17
12	11	30	7	18
13	12	31	7½	19
1	13	32	7¾	19.5
2	1	33	8¼	21
3	2	34.5	8½	21.5
4	3	36	8¾	22
5	4	37	9¼	23.5
6	5	38	9½	24
7	6	39	9¾	25

SHORT ROWS

Short rows are partial rows that are used to shape knitting without increases or decreases. In effect, by working only part of a row, you are building the depth of that part only. When working a short row, the pattern will indicate to wrap and turn (w&t). This means that you would wrap the next stitch (see below for instructions), which prevents a hole from forming at the turning point, and then turn your knitting. On the return row, the wraps are being picked up and worked together with their corresponding stitches to conceal the gap that the short row would otherwise create.

To wrap a knit stitch:

1. Work to where pattern indicates to wrap and turn (w&t). Slip next stitch onto right-hand needle and bring yarn forward.

2. Slip the now-wrapped stitch back onto left-hand needle, turn work, and continue following the pattern.

To wrap a purl stitch:

1. Work to where pattern indicates to wrap and turn. Slip next stitch onto right-hand needle and bring yarn to back.

2. Slip the now-wrapped stitch back onto left-hand needle, turn work, and continue following the pattern.

To pick up a wrap on the right side:

1. Work to wrapped stitch and slip it onto the right-hand needle.

2. With the tip of the left-hand needle, pick up the wrap from the right side of knitting and lift it over the top of its stitch, placing the wrap behind it (as it looks from the RS).

3. Work the wrap together with its corresponding stitch.

To pick up a wrap on the wrong side:

1. Work to wrapped stitch.

2. With the tip of the right-hand needle, pick up the wrap from the right side of knitting and lift it over the top of its stitch, placing the wrap in front of it (as it looks from the WS).

3. Insert left needle and knit the wrap and the stitch together.

CROSSING STITCHES

This technique can be used to eliminate little holes at the base of the thumb on mittens and heel joints on socks. On the round following the pick-up of the stitches from holder, work to 1 stitch before the gap and cross 2 stitches around that gap as follows:

- To cross 2 stitches to the right: insert right-hand needle into 2nd stitch from the front and knit without slipping it off the needle, then knit 1st stitch as usual and slip both stitches off the left-hand needle together.
- To cross 2 stitches to the left: insert right-hand needle into 2nd stitch from the back and knit without slipping it off the needle, then knit 1st stitch as usual and slip both stitches off the left-hand needle together.

THREE-NEEDLE BIND OFF

Place the stitches to be joined onto separate needles held parallel to each other and with right sides facing. Insert a third needle into the first stitch on both front and back needles and knit them together. *Knit 2 stitches together using 1 stitch from the front and 1 stitch from the back needle again; bind off 1 stitch from the right-hand needle as you would normally when binding off. Repeat from * until all stitches have been worked.

KITCHENER STITCH

The kitchener stitch, also known as grafting, is used to join live stitches without leaving a visible seam. Place stitches to be joined on parallel needles with wrong sides facing each other and thread a length of yarn onto a yarn needle.

1. Insert yarn needle into 1st stitch on front needle as if to purl, pull yarn through. Leave stitch on needle.
2. Insert yarn needle into 1st stitch on back needle as if to knit, pull yarn through. Leave stitch on needle.
3. Insert yarn needle into 1st stitch on front needle as if to knit, pull yarn through. Slip this stitch off needle.
4. Insert yarn needle into next stitch on front needle as if to purl, pull yarn through. Leave stitch on needle.
5. Insert yarn needle into 1st stitch on back needle as if to purl, pull yarn through. Slip this stitch off needle.
6. Insert yarn needle into next stitch on back needle as if to knit, pull yarn through. Leave this stitch on needle.

Repeat steps 3–6 until no stitches remain on needles.

COLORWORK KNITTING

Colorwork knitting uses two different strands of yarn in the same row or round to create pattern. On the chart each square represents a stitch of the corresponding color on your needles. The yarn strand that is not being used should always be carried behind work, this strand of yarn creates a float on the wrong side of knitting. Always carry the floats loosely in the back.

Depending on the yarn you use for your colorwork project, on longer stretches of pattern repeats you might want to weave the floats every few stitches over or under a stitch on the wrong side of the knitting.

To weave in yarn you carry from the left: insert your needle into the next stitch and under the unused yarn, knit your stitch as usual.

To weave in yarn you carry from the right: insert your needle into the next stitch and bring the unused yarn over your working needle (without knitting it), knit your stitch and unwrap or slip the unused yarn off the needle placing it behind work again.

WEAVING IN ENDS

To secure yarn tails on the wrong side of knitting, follow these steps.

1. With the wrong side facing you, thread the yarn tail into yarn needle.
2. Working away from the place where the yarn is attached to the fabric, pick up approximately 5 or 6 purl bumps on the diagonal.
3. Working in the opposite direction, pick up the same number of purl bumps that are placed directly under the ones you just used.
4. Repeat step 3 once more, cut yarn, leaving about a half-inch of yarn exposed on the wrong side.

Care instructions

Always read care instructions on the ball band before washing your hand knits. Any wools that are not superwash should be washed by hand. Most superwash wools, cottons, and synthetic fibers can be machine washed on a gentle cycle, although it is always advisable to hand-wash hats and scarves to prevent stretching.

To hand-wash your item, soak it in tepid water with mild detergent and leave to rest. If there is visible dirt on the item, rub it very gently, taking care not to agitate the fibers too much as this can cause felting. Squeeze out excess water, lay your item flat on a dry towel, roll it up, and press out as much water as you can. Place the item on a dry towel and ease it into shape while it's still damp. Do not stretch ribbing.

HEAD THINGS

THIRLWALL

This cap's highly textural fabric is created using basic knit and purl stitches worked in combination. The stitch pattern is echoed in the envelope-fold crown, adding just the right amount of slouch to the hat.

And as with most knit and purl textures, this one is completely reversible. No matter how many times this hat gets turned inside out, it always looks great.

SKILL LEVEL

Intermediate difficulty – Knit, purl, working in the round.

SIZES

Finished circumference 15¾ (18, 20¼, 22½) in / 40 (45.5, 51.5, 57) cm. Shown in size 18 in.

To fit head circumference 18 (20, 22, 24) in / 45.5 (51, 56, 61) cm.

MATERIALS AND NOTIONS

2 balls of Debbie Bliss Rialto DK (100% superwash merino wool; 115 yds / 105m per 50g ball); #23035.

US #6 (4mm) short circular needles or a set of dpns. Adjust needle size as needed to obtain correct gauge.

Stitch marker, spare needle for three-needle bind off, yarn needle.

GAUGE

23 sts and 36 rnds = 4 in / 10 cm in stitch pattern after blocking.

STITCH PATTERN

(Worked in multiples of 13 sts.)
Rnds 1–2: Purl.

Rnds 3–6: [K10, p3] around.
Rnds 7–8: Purl.
Rnds 9–12: [K1, p3, k9] around.
Rep Rnds 1–12 for pattern unless noted otherwise.

PATTERN

BODY

CO 90 (104, 116, 130) sts, pm and join to work in the round.

Set up rib: [K1, p1] around.
Work in rib as set for 2 (2, 3, 3) more rnds.

Next rnd: Pfb 1 (0, 1, 0) times, purl to end. 91 (104, 117, 130) sts.

Work Rnds 2–12 of the stitch pattern. Continue working stitch pattern, repeating Rnds 1–12 until hat measures 8½ (9, 10, 11) in / 21.5 (23, 25.5, 28) cm, ending with Rnd 6 or 12 of the stitch pattern.

Next rnd: Purl and adjust the number of sts to 92 (104, 116, 128).

CROWN

Distribute sts as follows to finish the crown: *place next 23 (26, 29, 32) sts on dpn, place next 23 (26, 29, 32) sts on waste yarn; rep from * once more.

Place needles parallel to each other and using a spare needle work 3-needle bind off over 23 (26, 29, 32) pairs of sts. Cut yarn.

Place sts from the waste yarn onto separate dpns, hold them together, and using a spare needle work 3-needle bind off over rem 23 (26, 29, 32) sts pairs of sts. Cut yarn.

FINISHING

Weave in ends and block if desired according to the ball band instructions.

NORTHUMBERLAND

This classic beanie can suit any child. Knit it in closely related colors (like those seen here) for a kid who doesn't like fussy clothes. Knit it in wildly contrasting brights for the kid who loves to make a statement. Or try the child's favorite sports team's colors.

No matter how you slice it, you've got a classic accessory that's both easy to wear and a great introduction to colorwork.

SKILL LEVEL

Intermediate difficulty – Knit, purl, colorwork, working in the round, simple decreases.

SIZES

Finished circumference 16 (17¼, 18¾, 20, 21¼) in / 40.5 (44, 47.5, 51, 54) cm. Shown in size 16 in (pale blue) and 17¼ in (navy).

To fit head circumference 18 (19½, 21, 22, 23½) in / 45.5 (49, 53, 56, 59) cm.

MATERIALS AND NOTIONS

1 skein each of Blue Sky Alpacas Sport Weight (100% baby alpaca; 110yds / 101m per 50g skein); #533 dark blue & #508 grey.

1 skein of Blue Sky Alpacas Melange (100% baby alpaca; 110yds / 101m per 50g skein); #800 light blue.

In the samples shown, the above yarns are used alternately as the MC (main color), color A (zigzag color), and color B (straight stripe color).

US #2½ (3mm) short circular needles or a set of dpns.
US #4 (3.5mm) short circular needles or a set of dpns. Adjust needle size as needed to obtain correct gauge.

Stitch markers and yarn needle.

GAUGE

24 sts and 32 rnds = 4 in / 10 cm in St st.

PATTERN

With A and smaller needles, CO 96 (104, 112, 120, 128) sts, pm and join to work in the round.

Set up rib rnd: [K2, p2] around. Cut yarn.

Change to B and work 2 rounds of 2×2 rib as set by the previous rnd. Cut yarn.

Change to MC and work as set until rib measures 1 in / 2.5 cm.

BODY

Change to larger needles. With MC, knit 3 rnds.

Work chart over the following 10 rnds. Cut A and B, leaving tails long enough to weave in ends.

With MC, work in St st until hat measures 4 (4¼, 4½, 4¾, 5) in / 10 (11, 11.5, 12, 12.5) cm from cast on.

CROWN

Size 16: Begin crown dec's at Rnd 9 below.
Size 17¼: Begin crown dec's at Rnd 7 below.
Size 18¾: Begin crown dec's at Rnd 5 below.
Size 20: Begin crown dec's at Rnd 3 below.
Size 21¼: Begin crown dec's at Rnd 1.

Rnd 1: [K2tog, k14] around. 120 sts.
Rnd 2 and every even-numbered rnd through 28: Knit.
Rnd 3: [K2tog, k13] around. 112 sts.
Rnd 5: [K2tog, k12] around. 104 sts.
Rnd 7: [K2tog, k11] around. 96 sts.
Rnd 9: [K2tog, k10] around. 88 sts.
Rnd 11: [K2tog, k9] around. 80 sts.
Rnd 13: [K2tog, k8] around. 72 sts.
Rnd 15: [K2tog, k7] around. 64 sts.

Rnd 17: [K2tog, k6] around. 56 sts.
Rnd 19: [K2tog, k5] around. 48 sts.
Rnd 21: [K2tog, k4] around. 40 sts.
Rnd 23: [K2tog, k3] around. 32 sts.
Rnd 25: [K2tog, k2] around. 24 sts.
Rnd 27: [K2tog, k1] around. 16 sts.
Rnd 29: [K2tog] around. 8 sts.

FINISHING

Cut yarn, leaving a long tail; thread tail through remaining sts. Weave in all ends and block lightly following the ball band instructions.

SIMONSIDE

This simple, chunky, ribbed hat sports a distinctive cable on one side. It's just enough cable to suggest the wings of Mercury – and just enough to introduce a new cable knitter to the joys of moving stitches around.

SKILL LEVEL

Intermediate difficulty – Knit, purl, simple cabling, working in the round, simple decreases.

SIZES

Finished circumference 16 (17¾, 19½, 21¼, 22¼) in / 40.5 (45, 49.5, 54, 56.5) cm. Shown in size 19½ in.

To fit head circumference 18 (20, 21.5, 23, 24) in / 45.5 (51, 54.5, 58.5, 61) cm.

MATERIALS AND NOTIONS

2 balls of Jil Eaton MinnowMerino (100% superwash merino; 77 yds / 70m per 50g skein); #01161.

US #8 (5mm) circular needles or a set of dpns. Adjust needle size as needed to obtain correct gauge.

Stitch marker, yarn needle.

GAUGE

18 sts and 25 rnds = 4 in / 10 cm in 2×2 rib pattern, measured slightly stretched.

PATTERN

BODY

CO 72 (80, 88, 96, 100) sts, pm, and join to work in the round.

Set up rib: [K2, p2] around.
Work in rib as set 1 (2, 3, 4, 4) more rnds.

Next rnd: Work cable pattern (see chart, next page) over 14 sts, p2, [k2, p2] to end.

Rep previous rnd until all pattern rows of chart have been worked.

Next rnd: [K2, p2] around.
Work as set by the prev rnd until hat measures 4¼ (4¾, 5¼, 5¾, 6) in / 11 (12, 13.5, 14.5, 15) cm.

CROWN

Dec rnd 1: [K2, p2tog] around. 54 (60, 66, 72, 75) sts.

Next rnd: [K2, p1] around.
Rep last rnd 4 times more.

Dec rnd 2: [K2tog, p1] around. 36 (40, 44, 48, 50) sts.

Next rnd: [K1, p1] around.
Rep last rnd 3 times more.

Dec rnd 3: [K2tog] around. 18 (20, 22, 24, 25) sts.
Continue working k2tog until 12 sts rem on the needles.

FINISHING

Cut yarn, leaving a long tail. Thread the tail through remaining sts to cinch. Weave in ends and block if desired according to the ball band instructions.

CABLE PATTERN
(Worked over 14 sts.)

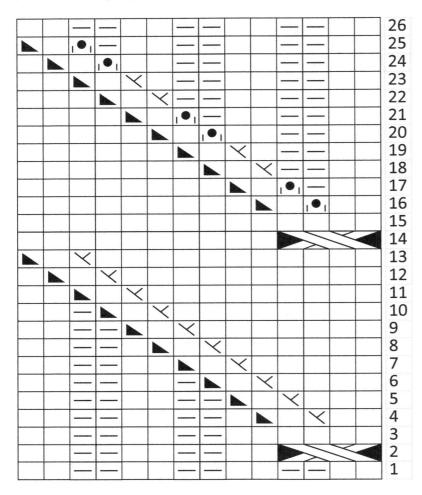

Legend

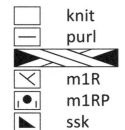

knit

— purl

C4L – sl2 onto cable needle (cn) and hold to front, k2, k2 from cn

⟨ m1R

⟨•⟩ m1RP

◣ ssk

DUERGAR

For your child's next hat, try this interesting take on a classic ribbed beanie. The crown was inspired by the raglan construction of a sweater shoulder and is shaped from the sides inwards instead of the usual spiral.

SKILL LEVEL

Intermediate difficulty – Knit, purl, working in the round, simple decreases.

SIZES

Finished circumference 14¼ (16, 17¾, 19½, 21¼) in / 36 (40.5, 45, 49.5, 54) cm. Shown in size 17¾ in.

To fit head circumference 16 (18, 20, 22, 24) in / 40.5 (45.5, 51, 56, 61) cm.

MATERIALS AND NOTIONS

1 ball of Knit Picks Swish Worsted (100% superwash merino wool, 110 yds / 101m per 50g ball); #24297 Allspice.

US #7 (4.5mm) short circular needles or a set of dpns. Adjust needle size as needed to obtain correct gauge.

Stitch markers, yarn needle, spare needle for 3-needle bind off.

GAUGE

18 sts and 26 rnds = 4 in / 10 cm in St st.

PATTERN

CO 64 (72, 80, 88, 96) sts, pm and join to work in the round.

Set up rib: [P1, k1 tbl] around.

Rep last rnd until brim measures 1 (1, 1¼, 1¼, 1½) in / 2.5 (2.5, 3, 3, 4) cm.

BODY

Set up body pattern: *[P1, k1 tbl] 5 (6, 7, 8, 9) times, p1, pm, k21 (23, 25, 27, 29), pm; rep from * to end.

Work as set by the previous rnd, keeping front and back panels in St st and side panels in Twisted Rib, until hat measures 4 (4¼, 4½, 4¾, 5) in / 10 (11, 11.5, 12, 12.5) cm from cast on.

CROWN

Next rnd: Work each stitch as it presents itself (keeping front and back panels in St st and side panels in Twisted Rib) to last 2 sts.

Dec rnd: *Place new marker, work cdd, removing previous marker, work to 2 sts before next marker as set; rep from * 3 times more, knit to end.

Repeat last 2 rnds 4 (5, 6, 7, 8) more times. 1 stitch rem on each side panel, 11 sts rem on each front St st panel.

Mark both side panel sts with a removable marker.

FINISHING

Turn the hat inside out and place all sts parallel to each other on two needles. Slip the marked stitch on to a third (working) needle ready to work a 3-needle bind off as follows:

*With your third needle, k2tog – 1 st from each front and back needle – you should have 2 sts on your working needle. BO 1 st. Repeat this step, from * until you have 1 st rem on either front or back needle, BO rem sts.

Weave in all ends and block if desired according to the ball band instructions.

WYLAM

This hat resulted from my self-imposed challenge to design a "different" ribbed beanie. I loved playing with the twisted stitch ribbing to make it integrate neatly into both the brim and the crown shaping of the hat. As a bonus, the pattern is written for both worsted- and bulky-weight yarns.

SKILL LEVEL

Intermediate difficulty – Knit, purl, working in the round, simple decreases.

SIZES

Finished circumference in worsted: 16 (17½, 19, 20¼, 21¾) in / 40.5 (44.5, 48.5, 51.5, 55) cm. Shown in size 16 in Cedar.

Finished circumference in bulky: 16 (17¾, 19½, 21¼) in / 40.5 (45, 49.5, 54) cm. Shown in size 17¾ in Brick.

The hat is intended to fit with about 2–3 in / 5–7.5 cm of negative ease.

MATERIALS AND NOTIONS

WORSTED-WEIGHT VERSION

1 skein of Lorna's Laces Shepherd Worsted (100% superwash merino wool; 225yds / 206m per 114g skein); Cedar.

US #7 (4.5mm) short circular needles or a set of dpns. Adjust needle size as needed to obtain correct gauge.

BULKY-WEIGHT VERSION

1 skein of Lorna's Laces Shepherd Bulky (100% superwash merino wool; 140yds / 128m per 114g skein); Brick.

US #10 (6mm) short circular needles or a set of dpns. Adjust needle size as needed to obtain correct gauge.

BOTH VERSIONS

Stitch markers; yarn needle.

GAUGE

22 sts and 30 rnds = 4 in / 10 cm in Rib pattern in worsted-weight yarn slightly stretched.

18 sts and 23 rnds = 4 in / 10 cm in Rib pattern St in bulky-weight yarn slightly stretched.

PATTERN

Worsted-weight version:
CO 88 (96, 104, 112, 120) sts, pm, and join to work in the round.

Bulky-weight version:
CO 72 (80, 88, 96) sts, pm, and join to work in the round.

Both versions:
Set up rib rnd: *[K1 tbl, p1] twice, k1 tbl, p3; rep from * to end.
Work as set until Rib measures 1 in / 2.5 cm. Take marker off, k1 tbl, p3, replace marker.

BODY

Next rnd: *[K1 tbl, p1] twice, k1 tbl, p3; rep from * to end.

Worsted-weight version:
Work as set by the previous rnd until hat measures 4¼ (4½, 5, 5½, 6) in / 11 (11.5, 12.5, 14, 15) cm from cast on.

Bulky-weight version:
Work as set by the previous rnd until hat measures 4¼ (4¾, 5¼, 5¾) in / 11 (12, 13.5, 14.5) cm from cast on.

CROWN

For crown shaping, all sizes follow the instructions in the left-hand column. At the end of each rnd, you should have the stitch count listed for your size in the table.

	WORSTED-WEIGHT SIZES					BULKY-WEIGHT SIZES			
INSTRUCTIONS	Size 16"	17½"	19"	20¼"	21¾"	16"	17¾"	19½"	21¼"
Rnd 1: [Ssk, k1 tbl, p1, k1 tbl, p3] around.	77	84	91	98	105	63	70	77	84
Rnd 2 and all even-numbered rnds through 14: Work each st as it presents itself.	(Same as previous rnd.)								
Rnd 3: [Ssk, p1, k1tbl, p3] around.	66	72	78	84	90	54	60	66	72
Rnd 5: [Ssk, k1 tbl, p3] around.	55	60	65	70	75	45	50	55	60
Rnd 7: [Ssk, p3] around.	44	48	52	56	60	36	40	44	48
Rnd 9: [Ssk, p2] around.	33	36	39	42	45	27	30	33	36
Rnd 11: [Ssk, p1] around.	22	24	26	28	30	18	20	22	24
Rnd 13: Ssk around.	11	12	13	14	15	9	10	11	12

FINISHING

Cut yarn leaving a long tail, thread tail through rem sts to cinch. Weave in all ends and block lightly following the ball band instructions.

RAINTON

Unlike any other hat in this book, this beanie is worked from the top of the crown down towards the brim. After the body of the hat is finished and its front and back stitches are bound off, the earflaps are knitted down continuously. The subtle ribbing of knits and purls offers an opportunity to wear this hat either way out.

SKILL LEVEL

Intermediate difficulty – Knit, purl, working in the round, simple increases and decreases.

SIZES

Finished circumference 16 (18, 20, 22) in / 40.5 (45.5, 51, 56) cm. Shown in size 20 in Pearl Ten and size 18 in Sweet Grape.

To fit head circumference 18 (20, 22, 24) in / 45.5 (51, 56, 61) cm.

MATERIALS AND NOTIONS

1 skein of Malabrigo Merino Worsted (100% merino wool; 210yds / 192m per 100g skein); #69 Pearl Ten or #509 Sweet Grape.

US #6 (4mm) set of dpns. Adjust needle size as needed to obtain correct gauge.

Stitch markers; yarn needle.

GAUGE

20 sts and 32 rnds = 4 in / 10 cm in St st.

PATTERN

CROWN

CO 5 sts, pm, and join to work in the round. As the number of sts grows redistribute them over 3 or 4 needles evenly if working on dpns.

Rnd 1: Kfb around. 10 sts.
Rnd 2: Kfb around. 20 sts.

Rnd 3 and every following odd-numbered rnd through 21: Knit.

Rnd 4: [Kfb, k1] around. 30 sts.
Rnd 6: [Kfb, k2] around. 40 sts.
Rnd 8: [Kfb, k3] around. 50 sts.
Rnd 10: [Kfb, k4] around. 60 sts.
Rnd 12: [Kfb, k5] around. 70 sts.
Rnd 14: [Kfb, k6] around. 80 sts.
Size 18 only: Skip to Body instructions.

Rnd 16: [Kfb, k7] around. 90 sts.
Size 20 only: Skip to Body instructions.

Rnd 18: [Kfb, k8] around. 100 sts.
Size 22 only: Skip to Body instructions.

Rnd 20: [Kfb, k9] around. 110 sts.

BODY

Rnd 1: *P1, k7 (8, 9, 10); rep from * to end. 80 (90, 100, 110) sts.
Rnd 2: Knit.
Rep Rnds 1 & 2 until hat measures 4 (4¼, 4½, 4¾) in / 10 (11, 11.5, 12) cm from crown, ending with a Rnd 1.

EARFLAPS

Earflaps set-up rnd: K25 (28, 31, 34), BO 31 (35, 39, 43) sts, k17 (19, 21, 23), BO 7 (8, 9, 10) sts to m, remove m,

BO 8 (9, 10, 11) sts. 17 (19, 21, 23) sts rem for each earflap on opposite sides of the hat.

Row 1 (RS): K2, k2tog, k4 (5, 6, 7), p1, k4 (5, 6, 7), ssk, k2. 15 (17, 19, 21) sts.
Row 2: K2, purl to last 2 sts, k2.
Row 3: K2, k2tog, k3 (4, 5, 6), p1, k3 (4, 5, 6), ssk, k2. 13 (15, 17, 19) sts.

Row 4: K2, purl to last 2 sts, k2.
Row 5: K6 (7, 8, 9), p1, k6 (7, 8, 9).
Rep Rows 4 & 5 until earflap measures 2 (2, 2¼, 2¼) in / 5 (5, 5.5, 5.5) cm.

SHAPE EARFLAP

For size 18, begin with Row 7; for size 20, begin with Row 5; for size 22, begin with Row 3; for size 24, begin with Row 1.

Row 1: K2, k2tog, k5, p1, k5, ssk, k2. 17 sts.
Row 2: K2, purl to last 2 sts, k2.

Row 3: K2, k2tog, k4, p1, k4, ssk, k2. 15 sts.
Row 4: K2, purl to last 2 sts, k2.

Row 5: K2, k2tog, k3, p1, k3, ssk, k2. 13 sts.
Row 6: K2, purl to last 2 sts, k2.

Row 7: K2, k2tog, k2, p1, k2, ssk, k2. 11 sts.
Row 8: K2, purl to last 2 sts, k2.

Row 9: K2, k2tog, k1, p1, k1, ssk, k2. 9 sts.
Row 10: K2, purl to last 2 sts, k2.

Row 11: K2, k2tog, p1, ssk, k2. 7 sts.
Row 12: K2, purl to last 2 sts, k2.

Row 13: K2, CDD, k2. 5 sts.
Row 14: K2, p1, k2.

I-CORD AND FINISHING

The i-cord is worked on 2 dpns over rem 5 sts.

I-cord: *With RS facing, slide your sts to the working end of your needle. With yarn held tightly behind, knit 5 sts. Do not turn. Rep from * until i-cord measures approx 6½ in / 16.5 cm. Cut yarn and thread tail through rem sts.

Weave in all ends and block if desired following the ball band instructions.

BOWBURN

You won't need a cable needle to create the twists and turns in this hat's mock cable motif – it's all done with simple decreases and increases. The crown shaping grows naturally from the pattern below, taking the interlacing rib to its tip.

SKILL LEVEL

Intermediate difficulty – Knit, purl, working in the round, simple decreases.

SIZES

Finished circumference 15¼ (17½, 19¾, 21¾) in / 38.5 (44.5, 50, 55) cm. Shown in size 17½ in and size 19¾ in.

To fit head circumference 17½ (19½, 22, 24) in / 44.5 (49.5, 56, 61) cm.

MATERIALS AND NOTIONS

1 skein of Manos del Uruguay Silk Blend (30% silk, 70% extrafine merino, 300 yds / 270m per 100g skein); #2444 Orinocco.

US #5 (3.75mm) set of dpns or a short circular. Adjust needle size as needed to obtain correct gauge.

Stitch markers; yarn needle.

GAUGE

22 sts and 32 rnds = 4 in / 10 cm in St st.

PATTERN

CO 84 (96, 108, 120), pm, join for working in the round.

Rnds 1–8: *P3, k4 (5, 6, 7); rep from * to end.
Rnd 9: *P3, k4 (5, 6, 7), p2, k2tog, k3 (4, 5, 6), m1L; rep from * to end.

Rnd 10: *P3, k4 (5, 6, 7), p2, k5 (6, 7, 8); rep from * to end.
Rnd 11: *P3, k4 (5, 6, 7), p1, k2tog, k3 (4, 5, 6), m1L, k1; rep from * to end.

Rnd 12: *P3, k4 (5, 6, 7), p1, k6 (7, 8, 9); rep from * to end.
Rnd 13: *P3, k4 (5, 6, 7), k2tog, k3 (4, 5, 6), m1L, k2; rep from * to end.

Rnd 14: *P3, k11 (13, 15, 17); rep from * to end.
Rnd 15: *P3, k3 (4, 5, 6), k2tog, k3 (4, 5, 6), m1L, k3; rep from * to end.

Rnd 16: *P3, k11 (13, 15, 17); rep from * to end.
Rnd 17: *P3, k2 (3, 4, 5), k2tog, k3 (4, 5, 6), m1L, k4; rep from * to end.

Size 15¼ only: skip to Rnd 24.

Rnd 18: *P3, k– (13, 15, 17); rep from * to end.
Rnd 19: *P3, k– (2, 3, 4), k2tog, k– (4, 5, 6), m1L, k5; rep from * to end.

Size 17½ only: skip to Rnd 24.

Rnd 20: *P3, k– (–, 15, 17); rep from * to end.
Rnd 21: *P3, k– (–, 2, 3), k2tog, k– (–, 5, 6), m1L, k6; rep from * to end.

Size 19¾ only: skip to Rnd 24.

Rnd 22: *P3, k– (–, –, 17); rep from * to end.
Rnd 23: *P3, k– (–, –, 2), k2tog, k– (–, –, 6), m1L, k7; rep from * to end.

Rnd 24: *P3, k6 (7, 8, 9), p1, k4 (5, 6, 7); rep from * to end.
Rnd 25: *P3, k1, k2tog, k3 (4, 5, 6), m1L, p1, k4 (5, 6, 7); rep from * to end.

Rnd 26: *P3, k5 (6, 7, 8), p2, k4 (5, 6, 7); rep from * to end.
Rnd 27: *P3, k2tog, k3 (4, 5, 6), m1L, p2, k4 (5, 6, 7); rep from * to end.

Rnd 28–30: *P3, k4 (5, 6, 7); rep from * to end.
Rnd 31: *P3, k4 (5, 6, 7); rep from * 10 times more, p3, place new EOR marker (removing old marker when you come to it).

Rnd 32: *M1R, k3 (4, 5, 6), ssk, p2, k4 (5, 6, 7), p3; rep from * to end.
Rnd 33: *K5 (6, 7, 8), p2, k4 (5, 6, 7), p3; rep from * to end.

Rnd 34: *K1, m1R, k3 (4, 5, 6), ssk, p1, k4 (5, 6, 7), p3; rep from * to end.
Rnd 35: *K6 (7, 8, 9), p1, k4 (5, 6, 7), p3; rep from * to end.

Rnd 36: *K2, m1R, k3 (4, 5, 6), ssk, k4 (5, 6, 7), p3; rep from * to end.
Rnd 37: *K11 (13, 15, 17), p3; rep from * to end.

Rnd 38: *K3, m1R, k3 (4, 5, 6), ssk, k3 (4, 5, 6), p3; rep from * to end.
Rnd 39: *K11 (13, 15, 17), p3; rep from * to end.
Rnd 40: *K4, m1R, k3 (4, 5, 6), ssk, k2 (3, 4, 5), p3; rep from * to end.

Size 15¼ only: skip to Rnd 47.

Rnd 41: *K– (13, 15, 17), p3; rep from * to end.
Rnd 42: *K– (5, 5, 5), m1R, k– (4, 5, 6), ssk, k– (2, 3, 4), p3; rep from * to end.

Size 17½ only: skip to Rnd 47.

Rnd 43: *K– (–, 15, 17), p3; rep from * to end.
Rnd 44: *K– (–, 6, 6), m1R, k– (–, 5, 6), ssk, k– (–, 2, 3); rep from * to end.

Size 19¾: skip to Rnd 47.

Rnd 45: *K– (–, –, 17), p3; rep from * to end.
Rnd 46: *K– (–, –, 7), m1R, k– (–, –, 6), ssk, k– (–, –, 2); rep from * to end.

Rnd 47: *K4 (5, 6, 7), p1, k6 (7, 8, 9), p3; rep from * to end.
Rnd 48: *K4 (5, 6, 7), p1, m1R, k3 (4, 5, 6), ssk, k1, p3; rep from * to end.

Rnd 49: *K4 (5, 6, 7), p2, k5 (6, 7, 8), p3; rep from * to end.
Rnd 50: *K4 (5, 6, 7), p2, m1R, k3 (4, 5, 6), ssk, p3; rep from * to end.

Rnd 51–53: *K4 (5, 6, 7), p3; rep from * to end.
Rnd 54: *K4 (5, 6, 7), p3; rep from * to end, remove m, k4 (5, 6, 7), pm. 84 (96, 108, 120) sts.

CROWN

Rnd 1: *P3, k4 (5, 6, 7), p2, k2tog, k3 (4, 5, 6); rep from * to end. 78 (90, 102, 114) sts.
Rnd 2: *P3, k4 (5, 6, 7), p1, k2tog, k3 (4, 5, 6); rep from * to end. 72 (84, 96, 108) sts.

Rnd 3: *P3, k4 (5, 6, 7), k2tog, k3 (4, 5, 6); rep from * to end. 66 (78, 90, 102) sts.
Rnd 4: *P3, k3 (4, 5, 6), k2tog, k3 (4, 5, 6); rep from * to end. 60 (72, 84, 96) sts.

Rnd 5: *P3, k2 (3, 4, 5), k2tog, k3 (4, 5, 6); rep from * to end. 54 (66, 78, 90) sts.
Rnd 6: *P3, k1 (2, 3, 4), k2tog, k3 (4, 5, 6); rep from * to end. 48 (60, 72, 84) sts

Size 15¼ only: skip to Rnd 10.

Rnd 7: *P3, k– (1, 2, 3), k2tog, k– (4, 5, 6); rep from * to end. – (54, 66, 78) sts.

Size 17½ only: skip to Rnd 10.

Rnd 8: *P3, k– (–, 1, 2), k2tog, k– (–, 5, 6); rep from * to end. – (–, 60, 72) sts.

Size 19¾ only: skip to Rnd 10.

Rnd 9: *P3, k– (–, –, 1), k2tog, k– (–, –, 6); rep from * to end. – (–, –, 66) sts.

Rnd 10: *P3, k2tog, k3 (4, 5, 6); rep from * to end. 42 (48, 54, 60) sts.
Rnd 11: *P3, k4 (5, 6, 7) to last 7 (8, 9, 10) sts, p3, k3 (4, 5, 6), place new EOR marker here.

Rnd 12: *Ssk, p2, k3 (4, 5, 6); rep from * to end. 36 (42, 48, 54) sts.
Rnd 13: *Ssk, p1, k3 (4, 5, 6); rep from * to end. 30 (36, 42, 48) sts.
Rnd 14: *Ssk, k3 (4, 5, 6); rep from * to end. 24 (30, 36, 42) sts

Size 15¼ only: skip to Rnd 18.
Size 17½ only: skip to Rnd 17.
Size 19¾ only: skip to Rnd 16.
Size 21¾ only: proceed with Rnd 15.

Rnd 15: [Ssk, k5] around. 36 sts.
Rnd 16: [Ssk, k4] around. 30 sts.
Rnd 17: [Ssk, k3] around. 24 sts.
Rnd 18: [Ssk, k2] around. 18 sts.
Rnd 19: [Ssk, k1] around. 12 sts.
Rnd 20: Ssk around. 6 sts.

FINISHING

Cut yarn leaving a long tail; pull through rem sts and bring to back. Weave in all ends. Block if desired according to the ball band instructions.

COLDSTREAM

The knit-and-purl arrow pattern on this beanie extends flawlessly into the crown. This is a great textured knit for anyone who wants to venture a little beyond stockinette or classic ribbing.

SKILL LEVEL

Intermediate difficulty – Knit, purl, working in the round, simple decreases.

SIZES

Finished circumference 16 (18¾, 21¼) in / 40.5 (47.5, 54) cm. Shown in size 18¾ in.

To fit head circumference 18 (21, 23) in / 45.5 (53.5, 58.5) cm.

MATERIALS AND NOTIONS

1 ball of Cascade Yarns 220 Superwash (100% superwash wool; 220yds / 200m per 100g ball); #811 Como Blue.

US #7 (4.5mm) short circular needles or a set of dpns. Adjust needle size as needed to obtain correct gauge.

Stitch markers, yarn needle.

GAUGE

24 sts and 32 rnds = 4 in / 10 cm in Zigzag rib stitch pattern slightly stretched.

PATTERN

CO 96 (112, 128) sts, pm, and join to work in the round.
Set up rib rnd: [K1, p1] around.
Rep previous rnd 4 more times.

□ knit
⊟ purl
◢ k2tog
▲ Cdd – centered double decrease

BODY

Work Zigzag chart, repeating Rnds 1–6 until hat measures 4 (4½, 5) in / 10 (11.5, 12.5) cm from cast on.

CROWN

Work Rnds 1–23 of Crown chart.

FINISHING

Cut yarn, leaving a long tail, thread tail through remaining sts. Weave in all ends and block lightly following the ball band instructions.

ZIGZAG CHART

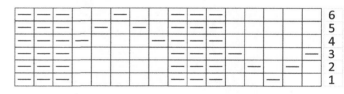

CROWN CHART

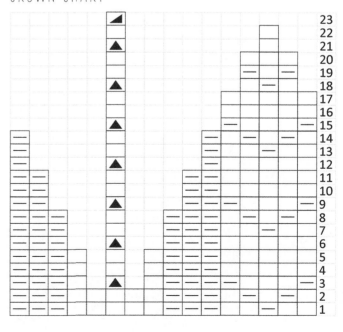

NECK THINGS

HARBOTTLE

Not everyone thinks of knitting cowls for children, but they are a great kids' accessory because they don't fall off – and they're perfect for going incognito!

The single-twist cables on this tube-shaped cowl create fun, geometrical flags across the surface. This plied and bouncy (and machine washable) wool translates well into cables, giving them perfect stitch definition.

SKILL LEVEL

Intermediate difficulty – Knit, purl, simple cabling, working in the round.

SIZES

Finished circumference 16 (17¾, 19½) in / 40 (45, 49.5) cm. Shown in size 16 in.

Finished height 7 (7¼, 7½) in / 18 (18.5, 19) cm.

MATERIALS AND NOTIONS

2 balls of Knit Picks Swish Worsted (100% superwash merino wool; 110 yds / 101m per 50g ball); #25631 Dove Heather.

US #7 (4.5mm) circular needles or a set of dpns. Adjust needle size as needed to obtain correct gauge.

3 stitch markers, yarn needle.

GAUGE

20 sts and 30 rnds = 4 in / 10 cm in St st.

STITCH PATTERNS

Stockinette stitch – Knit every rnd.
Flag pattern – See chart on next page.

PATTERN

CO 90 (99, 108) sts, pm, and join to work in the round.

Set up rib: [K1, p2] around.
Work in rib as set for 3 (4, 5) more rnds.

Set up stitch pattern: *K15 (18, 21), work chart base rnd, pm; rep from * twice more.

Next rnd: *K15 (18, 21), work Rnd 1 of flag chart; rep from * twice more.

Next rnd: *K15 (18, 21), work next rnd of flag chart; rep from * twice more.

Continue as set until chart is complete.

Set up rib: [K1, p2] around.
Work in rib as set for 3 (4, 5) more rnds.

BO loosely.

FINISHING

Weave in ends and block if desired according to the ball band instructions.

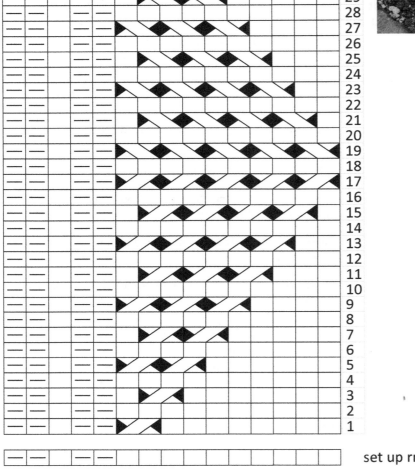

set up rnd

Legend

☐	knit
⊟	purl

C2R – cable 2 right – sl1 onto cable needle (cn) and hold to back, k1, k1 from cn.

TYNE GREEN

While cables are traditionally worked on a background of reverse stockinette (purl stitches), I love the more subtle texture that's created when you work those same cables on a stockinette ground (knit stitches). Worked in such a way they create a fluid texture that looks more like part of the fabric rather than braiding into a pattern atop of it.

SKILL LEVEL

Intermediate difficulty – Knit, purl, cabling, working in the round.

SIZES

Finished circumference 18 (20) in / 46 (51) cm, finished height 6 (6¼) in / 15 (16) cm. Shown in size 18 in.

MATERIALS AND NOTIONS

1 skein of Malabrigo Rios (100% superwash merino; 210 yds / 192m per 100g skein); # 37 Lettuce.

US #7 (4.5mm) circular needles or a set of dpns. Adjust needle size as needed to obtain correct gauge.

3 stitch markers, yarn needle.

GAUGE

20 sts = 4 in / 10 cm in St st.
Each cable patt repeat = 12 sts and 24 rnds = 2 in / 5 cm wide and 3½ in / 12.5 cm tall

STITCH PATTERNS

C6R (cable 6 sts to right): Slip 3 sts onto cn and hold to back, k3; k3 from cn.

C6L (cable 6 sts to left): Slip 3 sts onto cn and hold to front, k3; k3 from cn.

PATTERN

CO 100 (112) sts, pm, and join to work in the round. Work 3 (4) rnds in [k2, p2] rib.

Size 18 only:
Inc rnd: [K12, m1, k13, m1] around – 8 sts inc'd. 108 sts.
Size 20 only:
Inc rnd: [K14, m1] around – 8 sts inc'd. 120 sts.

Both sizes:
Rnds 1–4: Knit.
Rnd 5: [K6, C6R] around.

Rnds 6–10: Knit.
Rnd 11: [K6, C6R] around.

Rnd 12: Knit.
Rnd 13: [K3, C6R, k3] around.

Rnd 14: Knit.
Rnd 15: [C6R, k6] around.

Rnds 16–20: Knit.
Rnd 21: [C6R, k6] around.

Rnd 22: Knit.
Rnd 23: [K3, C6L, k3] around.

Rnd 24: Knit.
Rep Rnds 1–12 once more.

Size 18 only:
Dec rnd: [K11, k2tog, k12, k2tog] around – 8 sts dec'd. 100 sts.
Size 20 only:
Dec rnd: [K13, k2tog] around – 8 sts dec'd. 112 sts.

Both sizes:
Work 3 (4) rnds in [k2, p2] rib. Bind off sts loosely.

FINISHING

Weave in ends and block if desired according to the ball band instructions.

MALLARD

Scan the surface of any pond in England, and you are bound to spot the iridescent green head of a mallard duck. The Deep Sea colorway of Manos reminded me of that unmistakable, happy head bobbing in and out of the water in the spring. Worked from the bottom up with gentle shaping to follow body contour, the cowl splits at the lower end to prevent it from riding up and is finished with a perpendicular band at the top.

SKILL LEVEL

Intermediate difficulty – Knit, purl, short rows and working in the round.

SIZES

Finished circumference 17¼ (19¾) in / 44 (50) cm at the top; finished height 5½ (6) in / 14 (15) cm at the narrowest point. Shown in size 17¼ in.

MATERIALS AND NOTIONS

1 skein of Manos del Uruguay Wool Clasica (100% wool; 138yds/126m per 100g skein); # 7325 Deep Sea.

US #9 (5.5mm) short circular needle. Adjust needle size as needed to obtain correct gauge.

Stitch markers; yarn needle.

GAUGE

13 sts and 32 rnds = 4 in / 10 cm in garter stitch.

STITCH PATTERNS

Garter stitch knit in the round: Knit 1 rnd, purl 1 rnd.
Garter stitch knit flat: Knit every row.

PATTERN

SHORT-ROW TRIANGLE (MAKE 2)

CO 40 (44) sts, do not join.
Row 1: Knit to last 4 sts, w&t.

Row 2: Knit.
Row 3: Knit to 4 sts before the w&t, w&t.
Rep last 2 rows 7 (8) more times. 4 sts left unworked.

Place 2 triangles on a circular needle and knit 1 rnd, picking up the wraps as you come to them.

Work 5 rnds of garter stitch.

SHAPE FUNNEL TOP

Dec Rnd 1: [K8 (9), k2tog] around. 72 (80) sts.
Work 3 rnds of garter stitch.

Next rnd: [K7 (8), k2tog] around. 64 (72) sts.
Work 1 rnd of garter stitch.

Next rnd: [K6 (7), k2tog] around. 56 (64) sts.
Work in garter stitch until cowl measures 4½ (5) in / 11.5 (12.5) cm across the narrowest part, ending with a knit rnd.

TOP EDGING

Using a backward loop cast on, CO 4 sts and turn work.

Row 1: K3, ssk, turn.
Row 2: Bring yarn to back, sl1, k3, turn.
Rep last 2 rows until all sts have been worked. BO rem 4 sts.

FINISHING

Sew the top edging of the cowl together. Weave in ends and block if desired according to the ball band instructions.

CHECKERS

A moebius strip is a ribbon with half a twist added to it and ends connected into a loop in such a way that the resulting band has only one continuous surface and one edge.

To understand how it's done, try making your own moebius strip by cutting a long strip of paper about 2 inches wide, adding a half twist to one of its ends, and then taping the short ends into a continuous band. Now take a pencil and draw a line along its length. Amazing, no?

This property of a moebius strip lends itself beautifully to knitting in the round. The center line will be your starting point and you will be working from that line outwards in one continuous strip. Because the length of your knitting will literally double, you need to use a circular needle long enough to accommodate twice as many stitches as a cowl of this size would normally require. Once the cowl is finished, the lower double hem will give this piece extra stability and keep the twist in place.

SKILL LEVEL

Intermediate difficulty – Knit, purl, working in the round and moebius cast on.

SIZES

Finished circumference 18 (20) in / 46 (51) cm, finished height 9 in / 23 cm at the widest point. Shown in size 20 in.

MATERIALS AND NOTIONS

1 skein of Spud & Chloë Sweater (55% superwash wool, 45% organic cotton; 160yds / 146m per 100g skein); #7507 Moonlight.

US #7 (4.5mm) 20-inch and 40-inch long circular needles. Adjust needle size as needed to obtain correct gauge.

Stitch markers; crochet hook; yarn needle.

GAUGE

17 sts and 26 rnds = 4 in / 10 cm in 5×5 checkered stitch pattern.

STITCH PATTERNS

5×5 CHECKERED STITCH PATTERN

Rnds 1–5: [K5, p5] around.
Rnds 6–10: [P5, k5] around.

MOEBIUS CAST ON OPTION 1

Use Cat Bordhi's Moebius Cast On: www.youtube.com/watch?v=LVnTda7F2V4

MOEBIUS CAST ON OPTION 2

With a contrasting yarn and using a crochet hook, make a chain of the number of sts required for your size. Turn the chain over and with the circular needle, pick up and work Rnd 1 of the 5×5 Checkered stitch pattern into the back of the chain.

Next row: Carefully unpick the crochet chain stitch by stitch slipping the knit stitches that become exposed with the second end of the circular needle AT THE SAME TIME.

When this step is complete you will have the ends of the needle facing each other as to work in the round with the cable part forming a ring and threaded through the stitches twice. The cable part will be twisted within the stitches. The number of stitches will double.

PATTERN

Using either Moebius cast on option 1 or 2 above, CO 75 (85) sts and create a moebius loop. 150 (170) sts.

Pm to denote beg of round and work Rnds 4–10 of the 5×5 Checkered stitch pattern.

Work Rnds 1–10 of the 5×5 Checkered stitch pattern once, then Rnds 1–5 once.

Next rnd: BO 75 (85) sts. 75 (85) sts rem on the needle.

The bind off should stop directly above the beginning of the round marker and leaving you with half the original number of stitches.

Slip sts onto the short circular needle and, keeping the cable part of the needle not twisted, bring the ends together ready to work in the round. The cowl itself, however, will remain twisted.

EDGING

Knit 8 rnds, purl 1 rnd, knit 7 rnds. Bind off.

FINISHING

Fold hem in half and sew along the bind off to the base of the hem using whipstitch.

Weave in ends and block if desired according to the ball band instructions.

MILEFORTLET

Under Emperor Hadrian (117–138 CE), the Romans built a wall to barricade off the "barbarians." Now called Hadrian's Wall, the edifice runs through Northumberland National Park and beyond. After the wall stops in Bowness-on-Solway, regularly spaced forts called milefortlets continued to protect the perimeter.

Like its namesake, this scarf intersperses a knit-and-purl checkered landscape with garter band towers.

SKILL LEVEL

Simple difficulty – Knit and purl.

SIZES

60 in / 152.5 cm long × 6 in / 15 cm wide.

MATERIALS AND NOTIONS

3 skeins of Spud & Chloë Sweater (55% wool / 45% organic cotton; 160 yds / 146m per 100g skein), #7509 Firecracker.

US #8 (5mm) needles. Adjust needle size as needed to obtain correct gauge.

Yarn needle.

GAUGE

18 sts and 19 rows = 4 in / 10 cm in 3×3 Checkered stitch pattern.

STITCH PATTERNS

Garter stitch: knit every row.

3×3 Checkered stitch patt:
Row 1: [K3, p3] to last 3 sts, k3.
Row 2: [P3, k3] to last 3 sts, p3.
Row 3: [K3, p3] to last 3 sts, k3.
Rows 4 & 5: Knit.

Off-set rib:
Row 1: [K1, p1] to last st, k1.
Row 2: [P1, k1] to last st, p1.
Rows 3 & 4: Knit.

Note: To lengthen the scarf, work an extra repeat in each section between the garter bands. Each such increase will lengthen the scarf by approx 5½ in / 14 cm.

PATTERN

CO 27 sts.
Starting with a knit row, work 12 rows in garter stitch.

*Work 3×3 Checkered pattern 7 times.
Work 10 rows in garter stitch.
Work Off-set rib pattern 8 times.
Work 10 rows in garter stitch.

Rep from * twice more, then work 3×3 Checkered pattern 7 times and 10 rows of garter stitch.

BO all sts.

FINISHING

Weave in ends and block if desired according to the ball band instructions.

WOOLER

Variegated yarn seems to work so well with a simple garter stitch, highlighting the directionality of the knit piece. The main part of the scarf is worked straight up with a chevron stitch all along and is finished by working a strip of garter set against the scarf's length.

SKILL LEVEL

Intermediate difficulty – Knit stitches, short rows, simple increases and decreases.

SIZE

Finished size 54 in / 137 cm long × 5 in / 13 cm wide.

MATERIALS AND NOTIONS

2 skeins of Lorna's Laces Shepherd Worsted Multi (100% wool; 225yds / 206m per 100g skein); #901 Baltic Sea.

US #6 (4mm) long circular needle. Adjust needle size as needed to obtain correct gauge.

2 stitch markers; yarn needle.

GAUGE

15 sts and 36 rows = 4 in / 10 cm in garter stitch.

STITCH PATTERNS

Garter: knit every row.

PATTERN

CO 17 sts.
Row 1: Sl1, k7, pm, k9.
Row 2: Sl1, knit to end.

SHORT ROW WEDGE

Row 3: Sl1, k7, sm, k2, w&t.
Row 4: K1, m1R, k1, sm, m1L, k1, w&t. 19 sts.

Row 5: Knit to m, sm, k4, w&t.
Row 6: K3, m1R, k1, sm, m1L, k3, w&t. 21 sts.

Row 7: Knit to m, sm, k6, w&t.
Row 8: K5, m1R, k1, sm, m1L, k5, w&t. 23 sts.

Row 9: Knit to m, sm, k8, w&t.
Row 10: K7, m1R, k1, sm, m1L, k7, w&t. 25 sts.
Row 11: Knit to end of row.

SCARF BODY

Row 12: Sl1, k2tog, k9, m1R, k1, sm, m1L, k9, ssk, k1.
Row 13: Sl1, knit to end.
Rep last 2 rows for patt until scarf measures 54 in / 137 cm, or until desired length.

LEVEL UP THE TOP END

Row 1: Sl1, knit to 2 sts before m, w&t.
Row 2: Knit to last 3 sts, ssk, k1.

Row 3: Sl1, k7, w&t.
Row 4: Knit to last 3 sts, ssk, k1.

Row 5: Sl1, k5, w&t.
Row 6: Knit to last 3 sts, ssk, k1.

Row 7: Sl1, k3, w&t.
Row 8: Knit to last 3 sts, ssk, k1.

Row 9: Sl1, knit to m, sm, knit to end.
Row 10: Sl1, k2tog, knit to 3 sts before m, w&t.

Row 11: Knit.
Row 12: Sl1, k2tog, k5, w&t.

Row 13: Knit.
Row 14: Sl1, k2tog, k3, w&t.

Row 15: Knit.
Row 16: Sl1, k2tog, k1, w&t.

Row 17: Knit.
Rows 18 & 19: Remove m and knit across whole width.

BO all sts, don't cut yarn.

PERPENDICULAR GARTER PANEL

With long circular needle, pick up and knit 1 stitch into back of each loop along the long side of the scarf.

Knit 8 rows. Bind off loosely.

FINISHING

Weave in ends and block if desired according to the ball band instructions.

WETLAND

Double knitting is a technique that creates reversible fabric, with the pattern on one side typically being the reverse of the pattern on the flip side. Both the right and the wrong sides are worked simultaneously on the same set of needles, with front stitches (the ones that are facing you) always worked in stockinette as knits and the back stitches (those that are facing away from you) always worked in reversed stockinette as purls. The color stitch pattern itself is what holds the two sides together in a quilt-like fashion.

SKILL LEVEL

Intermediate difficulty – Knit stitches, increases and decreases.

SIZE

Finished size: 61 in / 155 cm long × 7 in / 18 cm wide.

MATERIALS AND NOTIONS

4 balls each of Debbie Bliss Rialto Aran (100% merino wool; 88 yds / 80m per 50g ball); #21236 and #21229.

US #8 (5mm) needles. Adjust needle size as needed to obtain correct gauge.

2 stitch markers; yarn needle.

GAUGE

18 sts and 20 rows = 4 in / 10 cm in St st.

PATTERN NOTES

READING DOUBLE KNITTING CHARTS

The squares on the chart represent stitches in pairs. For each knit stitch that creates the front fabric you will work a purl stitch that creates the back fabric. The yarn in double knitting should be carried in between the two layers; when working the front stitch the yarn is held in back, and when working the back stitch the yarn is held in front of it.

With MC being the main color and CC the contrast color, those stitches should be worked as follows: K1MC with yarn in back, p1CC with yarn in front. When the color in the chart changes, the stitches should be worked in a negative color as K1CC with yarn in back, p1MC with yarn in front.

EDGE STITCHES

The edge stitches of this scarf are worked with both MC and CC held together to keep the front and the back fabric joined. Worked in such a way, each edge stitch will consist of both MC and CC strands and count as one "double" stitch.

The first stitch of each row is simply slipped onto the RH needle without being worked. The last "double" stitch of each row is knit with two strands of yarn, MC and CC, held together.

WEAVING IN ENDS

Weaving in the ends is easiest if done as you change a ball of yarn rather than after the scarf is finished. When changing the ball, leave a tail long enough to be woven in, join yarns by making a loose knot and weaving in the end on the wrong (inside) side of the fabric before continuing knitting.

PATTERN

CO 32 sts with a strand each of yarn A and B held tog. Re-arrange sts on the needle so that each MC stitch is followed by CC stitch.

Work Chart 1.

Next row: Sl1, [k1MC, p1CC] to last st introducing 1 st of CC at random, k1 with 2 strands.
Next row: Sl1, [k1CC, p1MC] to last st, k1 with 2 strands.
Rep previous 2 rows until scarf measures 55 in / 140cm.

Work Chart 2.

BIND OFF

When binding off each pair of sts MC and CC are counted as one. Bind off sts as follows: Slip first st onto RH needle, *k2tog, bind off st on the RH needle; rep from * to end.

FINISHING

Weave in remaining ends hiding them between the layers of fabric or along the side stitch and block if desired according to the ball band instructions.

CHART 1

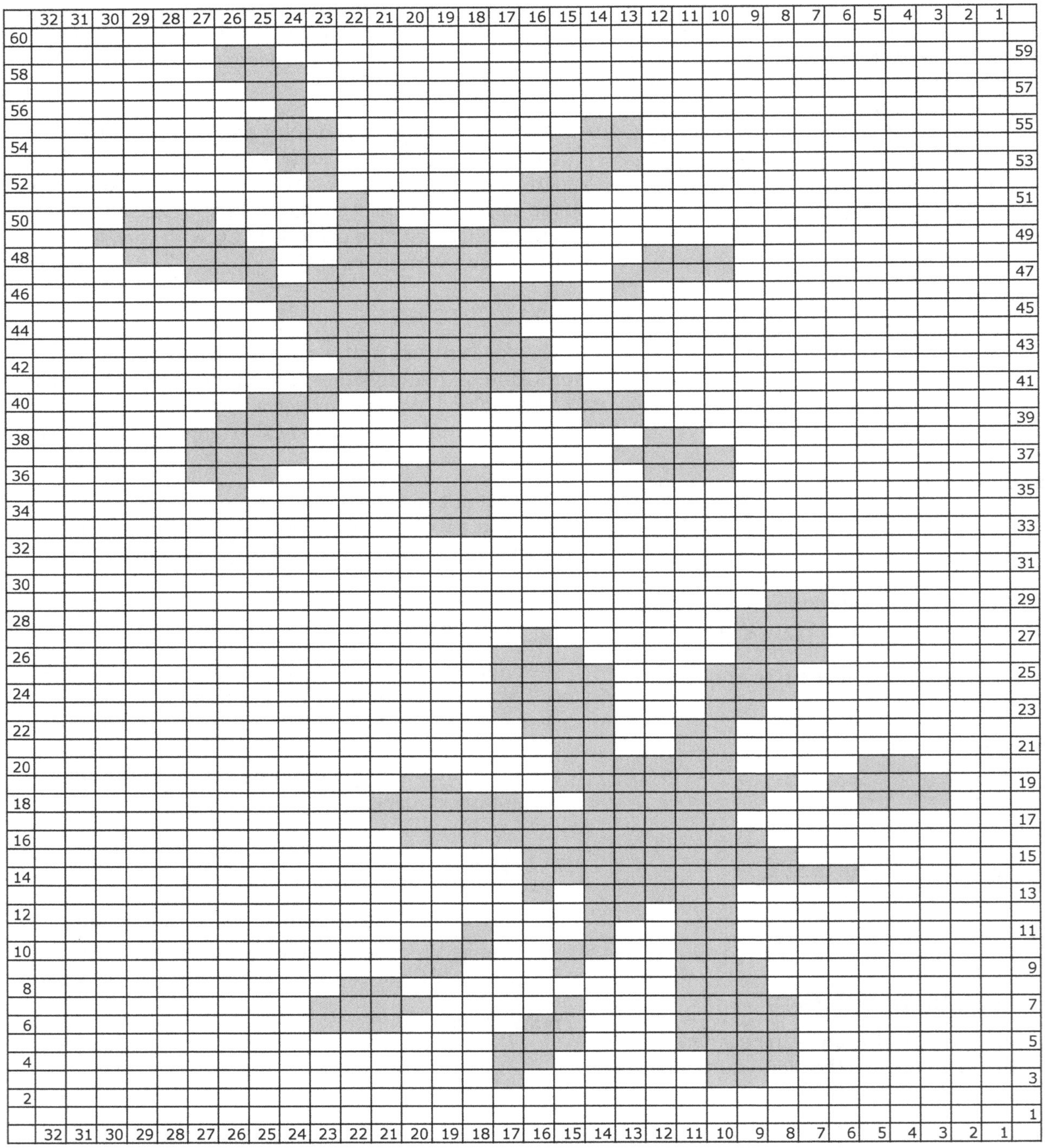

CHART 2

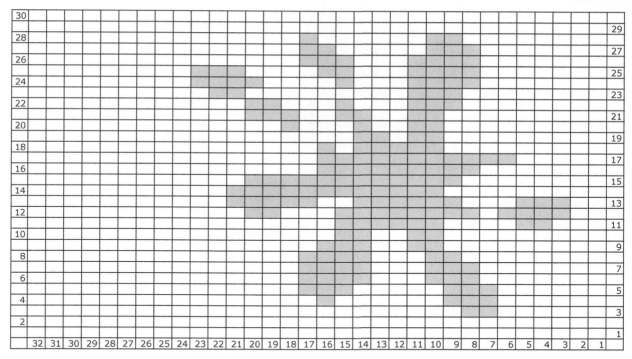

HAND THINGS

DOODLE GLOVES

The geometrical pattern for these gloves was inspired by some daft doodling my kids used to do to decorate their hands. The lice-stitch technique used here sprinkles single stitches of contrast color across the background, and is a clever way of carrying your contrasting yarn through the long stretches while working large, non-repeating motifs of colorwork.

You can make these gloves either with fingers or without. And as an added bonus, your kid can have a doodle on his or her hands without having to clean off the marker later.

SKILL LEVEL

Intermediate difficulty – Knit, purl, colorwork in the round, simple increases and decreases.

SIZES

Finished hand circumference: 5¼ (5¾, 6¼, 6¾, 7) in / 13.5 (14.5, 16, 17, 18) cm. Shown in size 5¼ in (fingerless mitts) and 6¼ in (gloves).

To fit approx age 3–4 (5–6, 7–8, 9–10, 10+) years old.

MATERIALS AND NOTIONS

1 skein each of Madelinetosh Tosh Sock (100% superwash merino wool; 395 yds / 361m per 100g skein), Black Currant and Mica.

(The pictured mitts were both knit from the above two skeins.)

US #1 (2.25mm) set of dpns. Adjust needle size as needed to obtain correct gauge.

Stitch markers, yarn needle.

GAUGE

36 sts and 38 rnds = 4 in / 10 cm in Lice pattern.

STITCH PATTERN

LICE PATTERN (MULT OF 4)

Rnd 1: [K1 CC, k3 MC] around.
Rnd 2: [K2 MC, k1 CC, k1 MC] around.
Rep Rnds 1 & 2 for pattern.

PATTERN

CUFF

With MC, CO 48 (52, 56, 60, 64) sts, pm and join to work in the round.

Set up rib: [K2, p2] around.
Join CC and work in 2×2 rib as set for 2 rnds. Cut CC.

Change to MC and work in 2×2 rib as set until cuff measures 2¼ in / 6 cm from cast on.

(See sidebar for fingerless glove hand instructions.)

LEFT HAND

Set up pattern: Work Rnd 1 of Lice patt over foll 24 (26, 28, 30, 32) sts, pm, work Rnd 1 of Left chart starting from row 5 (4, 3, 2, 1) over foll 24 (26, 28, 30, 32) sts.

FOR FINGERLESS GLOVES

HAND

Cut CC and work in [k2, p2] rib for 4 rnds. BO in pattern.

THUMB

Place 13 (15, 15, 17, 19) thumb sts onto dpns, join MC and pick up and knit 3 sts from the gap. 16 (18, 18, 20, 22) sts.

Work in [k1, p1] rib for 4 rnds. BO in pattern.

Next rnd: Work next rnd of Lice patt to marker, sm, work next rnd of Left chart to m.

Work as set by the last rnd until piece measures 3 in / 7.5 cm from cast on.

LEFT THUMB GUSSET

Rnd 1: Work next row of Lice patt to 1 st before m, pm, m1R, k1, m1L, sm, work next rnd of Left chart to m.

Rnd 2–3: Work even as set by the previous rnd.
Rnd 4: Work next row of Lice patt to m, sm, m1R, knit to m, m1L, sm, work next rnd of Left chart to m.

Rep Rnds 2–4 until there are 13 (15, 15, 17, 18) sts between thumb markers.

Next rnd: Work to m, place thumb sts onto a holder, CO 1 st, work next rnd of Left chart to m.

Work even as set by the previous rnd, keeping palm and thumb gusset sts in Lice stitch and back hand sts in Left chart, to the last row of the chart. Change to Lice pattern and work even for ½ (¾, ¾, 1, 1) in / 1.25 (2, 2, 2.5, 2.5) cm or to the base of index finger.

RIGHT HAND

Set up pattern: Work Rnd 1 of Right chart starting from row 5 (4, 3, 2, 1) over foll 24 (26, 28, 30, 32) sts, pm, work row 1 of Lice patt over foll 24 (26, 28, 30, 32) sts.

Next rnd: Work next rnd of Right chart to m, sm, work next row of Lice patt to m.

Work as set by the last rnd until piece measures 3 in / 7.5 cm from cast on.

RIGHT THUMB GUSSET

Rnd 1: Work next rnd of Right chart to m, sm, m1R, k1, m1L, pm, work next row of Lice patt to m.

Rnd 2–3: Work even as set by the previous rnd.
Rnd 4: Work next rnd of Right chart to m, sm, m1R, knit to m, m1L, sm, work next row of Lice patt to m.

Rep Rnds 2–4 until there are 13 (15, 15, 17, 19) sts between thumb markers.

Next rnd: Work next rnd of Right chart to m, place thumb sts onto a holder, CO 1 st, work to m.

Work even as set by the previous rnd, keeping palm and thumb gusset sts in Lice stitch and back hand sts in Right chart, to the last row of the chart. Change to Lice pattern and work even until hand measures ½ (¾, ¾, 1, 1) in / 1.25 (2, 2, 2.5, 2.5) cm or to the base of index finger.

FINGERS – WORK FOR BOTH HANDS

With the yarn attached at the beg of rnd, in the middle of what is going to be a pinky finger, cut CC and continue working in MC only. Keeping side markers intact, place all sts onto holder.

PINKY FINGER

Transfer 6 (6, 7, 7, 8) sts from the back of hand and 6 (6, 7, 7, 8) sts from the palm onto dpns. CO 2 sts, knit to m. 14 (14, 16, 16, 18) sts.

Work even in St st until finger is the desired length, approx 1¼ (1¼, 1½, 1½, 1¾) in / 3.5 (3.5, 4, 4, 4.5) cm.

Dec rnd: Work k2tog until 6 sts rem. Cut yarn, leaving a long tail, thread through rem sts and pull to cinch.

RING FINGER

Transfer 5 (6, 6, 7, 7) sts closest to the pinky finger on both the palm and the back of hand onto dpns. Join yarn and pick up and knit 2 sts from the cast-on base of the pinky finger, k5 (6, 6, 7, 7), CO 3 sts, k5 (6, 6, 7, 7). 15 (17, 17, 19, 19) sts.

Work even in St st until finger is the desired length, approx 1½ (1¾, 1¾, 2, 2¼) in / 4 (4.5, 4.5, 5, 5.5) cm.

Dec rnd: Work k2tog until 6 sts rem. Cut yarn, leaving a long tail, thread through rem sts and pull to cinch.

MIDDLE FINGER

Transfer 5 (6, 6, 7, 7) sts closest to the ring finger on both the palm and the back of hand onto dpns. Join yarn and pick up and knit 3 sts from the cast-on base of the ring finger, k5 (6, 6, 7, 7), CO 3 sts, k5 (6, 6, 7, 7). 16 (18, 18, 20, 20) sts.

Work even in St st until finger is the desired length, approx 1¾ (2, 2¼, 2½, 2¾) in / 4.5 (5, 5.5, 6, 7) cm.

Dec rnd: Work k2tog until 6 sts rem. Cut yarn, leaving a long tail, thread through rem sts and pull to cinch.

INDEX FINGER

Transfer rem 16 (16, 18, 18, 20) onto dpns. Join yarn and pick up and knit 3 sts from the cast-on base of the middle finger, k16 (16, 18, 18, 20). 18 (18, 20, 20, 22) sts.

Work even in St st until finger is the desired length, approx 1¾ (2, 2¼, 2½, 2¾) in / 4.5 (5, 5.5, 6, 7) cm.

Dec rnd: Work k2tog until 6 sts rem. Cut yarn, leaving a long tail, thread through rem sts and pull to cinch.

THUMB

(For fingerless mitt thumb instructions, see sidebar on first pattern page.)

Transfer 13 (15, 15, 17, 19) thumb sts onto dpns, join yarn and pick up and knit 3 sts from the gap. 16 (18, 18, 20, 22) sts.

Work even in St st until thumb is the desired length, approx 1 (1¼, 1½, 1¾, 2) in / 2.5 (3, 4, 4.5, 5) cm.

Dec rnd: Work k2tog until 6 sts rem. Cut yarn, leaving a long tail, thread through rem sts and pull to cinch.

FINISHING

Weave in all ends and block if desired following the ball band instructions.

NOTES FOR BOTH CHARTS (SEE NEXT PAGE):

- For size 5¼: Work orange outlined section only, Rows 5–32.
- For size 5¾: Work green outlined section only, Rows 4–32.
- For size 6¼: Work blue outlined section only, Rows 3–32.
- For size 6¾: Work red outlined section only, Rows 2–32.
- For size 7: Work entire chart, black outlined section, Rows 1–32.

RIGHT HAND CHART

LEFT HAND CHART

CHEVIOT HILLS

Spectacular views paired with the quiet of the country are the most rewarding parts of hiking for me. Darted with paths and trails, the Cheviots are one of those places that you escape to so you can catch the view of picturesque, rolling hills zigzagging in the horizon.

The single twists of cables in these mitts bring together knit and purl textures much like the Cheviot Hill valleys bridge the fields.

SKILL LEVEL

Intermediate difficulty – Knit, purl, working in the round, simple increases and decreases.

SIZES

Finished hand circumference 4¾ (5¼, 6, 6¾) in / 12 (13.5, 15, 17) cm. Shown in size 5¼ in.

To fit approx age 3–4 (5–6, 7–8, 9–10) years old.

MATERIALS AND NOTIONS

1 skein of Mirasol Tuhu (50% llama, 40% wool, 10% angora; 109 yds / 100m per 50g skein); #2004 Cool Blue.

US #4 (3.5mm) set of dpns. Adjust needle size as needed to obtain correct gauge.

Stitch markers, yarn needle

GAUGE

24 sts and 36 rnds = 4 in / 10 cm in St st.

PATTERN

CUFF

CO 28 (32, 36, 40) sts, pm and join to work in the round.
Set up rib: [K1, p1] around.
Work as set until Rib measures 1 (1¼, 1½, 1½) in / 2.5 (3, 4, 4) cm.

Next rnd: *K14 (16, 18, 20), pm, knit to end.

LEFT MITT

Set-up Rnd: K14 (16, 18, 20), sm, work Chart 1 across foll 14 (16, 18, 20) sts.

Size 4¾: start from Rnd 4; size 5¼: start from Rnd 3; size 6: start from Rnd 2; size 6¾: start from Rnd 1.

Next rnd: K12 (14, 16, 18), pm, k2, sm, knit to end.

LEFT THUMB GUSSET

Thumb increases are worked on either side of the first marker on every other rnd.

Rnd 1: Knit to 1 st before m, m1R, k1, sm, k1, m1L, knit to m, sm, work Chart 2 across foll 14 (16, 18, 20) sts.
Rnd 2: Knit to second m, sm, work Chart 2 across foll 14 (16, 18, 20) sts.
Rep Rnds 1 & 2 another 3 (3, 4, 5) times. 8 (8, 10, 12) sts inc'd. (To make the thumb gusset bigger, work Rnds 1 & 2 once again. 10 (10, 12, 14) sts.)

Next rnd: Knit to 5 (5, 6, 7) sts before m, slip next 10 (10, 12, 14) sts onto waste yarn, CO 2 sts, k1, sm, work Chart 2 to end.

RIGHT MITT

Set-up Rnd: Work Chart 2 across foll 14 (16, 18, 20) sts, sm, k14 (16, 18, 20).

Size 4¾: start from Rnd 4; size 5¼: start from Rnd 3; size 6: start from Rnd 2; size 6¾: start from Rnd 1.

Next rnd: K14 (16, 18, 20), sm, k2, pm, knit to end.

RIGHT THUMB GUSSET

Thumb increases are worked on either side of the second marker on every other rnd.

Rnd 1: Work Chart 1 across foll 14 (16, 18, 20) sts, sm, knit to 1 st before m, m1R, k1, sm, k1, m1L, knit to end.
Rnd 2: Work Chart 1 across foll 14 (16, 18, 20) sts, sm, knit to end.

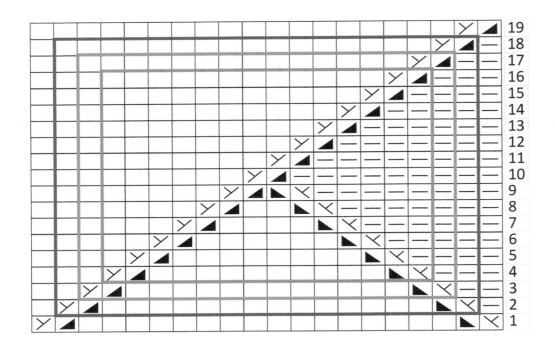

CHART 1

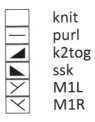

knit	
purl	
k2tog	
ssk	
M1L	
M1R	

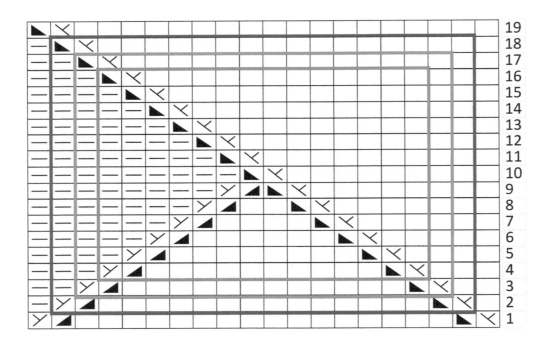

CHART 2

NOTES FOR BOTH CHARTS

- For size 4¾: Work red outlined section only, Rows 4–16.
- For size 5¼: Work green outlined section only, Rows 3–17.
- For size 6: Work blue outlined section only, Rows 2–18.
- For size 6¾: Work entire chart, Rows 1–19.

Rep Rnds 1 & 2 another 3 (3, 4, 5) times. 8 (8, 10, 12) sts inc'd. (To make the thumb gusset bigger, work Rnds 1 & 2 once again. 10 (10, 12, 14) sts.)

Next rnd: Work Chart 1 to m, sm, k1, slip foll 10 (10, 12, 14) sts onto waste yarn, CO 2 sts, knit to end.

BOTH MITTS

Work even, keeping palm sts in St st and working the back hand sts in Chart 1 for Right mitt or Chart 2 for Left mitt as set by the previous rnds until all chart rows have been worked.

Knit 2 rnds.

Work in [k1, p1] rib for 4 (4, 5, 5) rnds. BO in patt.

THUMB

Place 10 (10, 12, 14) thumb sts onto dpns, join yarn and pick up and knit 2 sts from the cast-on gap. 12 (12, 14, 16) sts.

Work in St st for 2 (4, 6, 8) rnds. Work in [k1, p1] rib for 3 rnds. BO in patt.

FINISHING

Weave in all ends and block lightly following the ball band instructions.

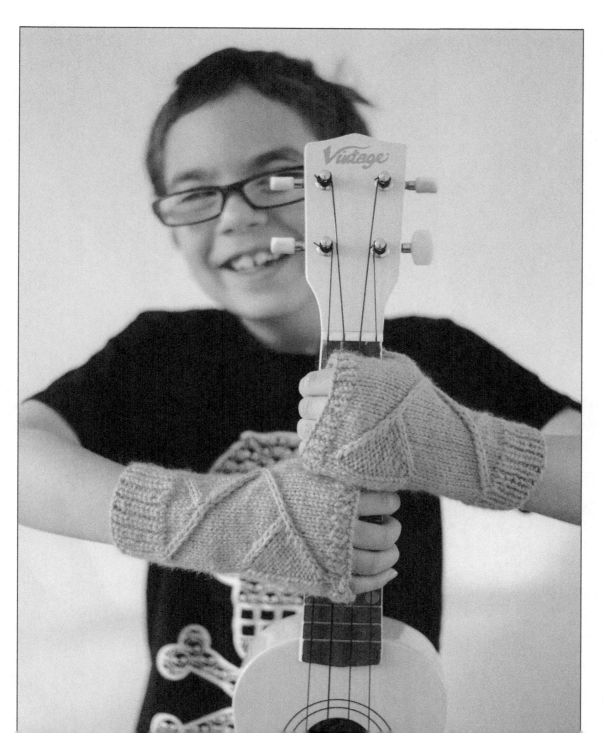

BACK HAND HITCH

Ribbed fingerless mitts with a braided cable flowing seamlessly in and out of the knit ridges.

SKILL LEVEL

Intermediate difficulty – Knit, purl, working in the round, cabling, simple increases.

SIZES

Finished hand circumference 6 (6¾, 7¼) in / 15 (17, 18.5) cm. Shown in size 6¾ in.

To fit approx age 4-5 (6-9, 10-12) years old.

MATERIALS AND NOTIONS

1 skein of Cascade Yarns 220 Superwash Sport (100% superwash merino wool; 136yds / 125m per 50g skein); #802 Green Apple.

US4 (3.5mm) set of dpns. Adjust needle size as needed to obtain correct gauge.

Stitch markers, yarn needle.

GAUGE

24 sts and 37 rnds = 4 in / 10 cm in 2×2 Rib pattern slightly stretched.

PATTERN

CUFF (BOTH HANDS)
CO 36 (40, 44) sts, pm, and join to work in the round.

Set up rib: [K2, p2] around.

Work as set until Rib measures 1½ (1¾, 2) in / 4 (4.5, 5) cm.

BOTH MITTS

Set up cable: Work Row 1 of cable chart over the next 18 sts, work to end in patt.

Next rnd: Work next row of cable chart over the next 18 sts, work to end in patt.

Continue as set by the last rnd until all 17 rows of the cable chart have been worked.

RIGHT THUMB GUSSET

Set up rnd: Work 18 (20, 22) sts in patt, pm, work 2 sts in patt, pm, work to end in patt. (Skip to "Both Mitts" section below.)

LEFT THUMB GUSSET

Set up rnd: Work 18 sts in patt, place new EOR marker, work 16 (18, 20) sts in patt, pm, work 2 sts in patt, pm, work to end in patt.

BOTH MITTS

Gusset increases are worked within the markers.

Rnd 1: Work as set to m, sm, m1L, work 2 sts in patt, m1R, work to end in patt.
Rnd 2: Work each stitch as it presents itself.

Rep Rnds 1 & 2 another 3 (3, 4) times. 10 (10, 12) sts between markers.

Next rnd: Work in patt to m, remove marker and place thumb sts onto waste yarn, CO 2 sts, remove second marker, work in patt to end.

Work in 2×2 rib as set until the hand measures 1 (1¼, 1½) in / 2.5 (3, 3.5) cm from the end of the thumb gusset. Bind off.

THUMB

Place 10 (10, 12) sts held on waste yarn onto 2 dpns, join yarn and pick up and knit 2 sts from the base of the hand cast on.

Work as set for ½ in / 1.5cm. Bind off loosely.

FINISHING

Weave in all ends and block lightly following the ball band instructions.

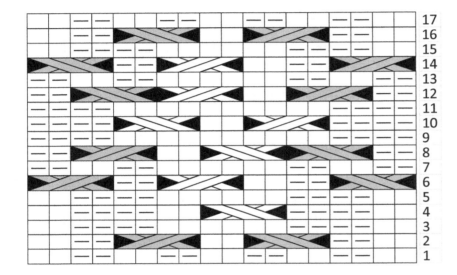

Legend

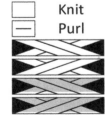

	Knit
—	Purl

C4L – cable 4 sts left – Sl2 onto cable needle (cn) and hold to front, k2, k2 from cn.
C4R – cable 4 sts right – Sl2 onto cn and hold to back, k2, k2 from cn.
C4LP – cable 4 sts left purl – Sl2 onto cn and hold to front, p2, k2 from cn.
C4RP – cable 4 sts right purl – Sl2 onto cn and hold to back, k2, p2 from cn.

DABBLER

This stockinette stitch mitten is yet another wardrobe staple for anyone in the family. Mittens are always a win: younger children don't have to struggle to fit into each separate glove finger, while older kids love wearing mittens over their gloves for a snowball fight.

SKILL LEVEL

Intermediate difficulty – Knit, purl, working in the round, simple increases and decreases.

SIZES

Finished hand circumference 5¾ (6½, 7¼) in / 14.5 (16.5, 18.5) cm. Shown in size 5¾ in.

To fit approx age 4–5 (6–9, 10–12) years old.

MATERIALS AND NOTIONS

1 skein of Lorna's Laces Shepherd Worsted (100% superwash merino wool; 225yds / 206m per 100g skein); Cranberry.

US #4 (3.5mm) set of dpns.
US #5 (3.75mm) set of dpns.
Adjust needle size as needed to obtain correct gauge.

Stitch markers; yarn needle.

GAUGE

22 sts and 29 rnds = 4 in / 10 cm in St st on larger needles.

PATTERN

CUFF

With smaller needles, CO 32 (36, 40) sts, pm, and join to work in the round.

Set up rib: [K2, p2] around.

Work as set until Rib measures 2¾ (3, 3½) in / 7 (7.5, 9) cm. Change to larger needles.

RIGHT MITTEN

Next rnd (set up patt): Work Row 1 (3, 5) of Right chart patt over 12 sts, knit to end.

Next rnd: Work next row of Right chart patt over 12 sts, knit to end.

Note: Continue working chart through thumb gusset and hand until all 22 rows have been worked, change to St st for the rest of the hand after that.

Thumb gusset set-up rnd: Work chart over next 12 sts, k4 (6, 8), pm, k1, pm, knit to end.

LEFT MITTEN

Next rnd (set up patt): K20 (24, 28), work Row 1 (3, 5) of Left chart patt over 12 sts.

Next rnd: K20 (24, 28), work next row of Left chart patt over 12 sts.

Note: Continue working chart through thumb gusset and hand until all 22 rows have been worked, change to St st for the rest of the hand after that.

Thumb gusset set-up rnd: K15 (17, 19), pm, k1, pm, k4 (6, 8), work chart over next 12 sts.

BOTH MITTENS

Gusset increases are worked within the markers.

Rnd 1: Work in patt to m, sm, m1L, knit to m, m1R, sm, work in patt to end. 2 sts inc'd.
Rnd 2: Work each stitch as it presents itself.
Rep previous 2 rnds 3 (4, 5) more times. 9 (11, 13) sts between markers.

Next rnd: Work in patt to m, remove m, and place thumb sts onto waste yarn, CO 1 st, remove second m, work in patt to end. 32 (36, 40) sts.

RIGHT MITTEN CHART

22
21
20
19
18
17
16
15
14
13
12
11
10
9
8
7
6
5
4
3
2
1

LEFT MITTEN CHART

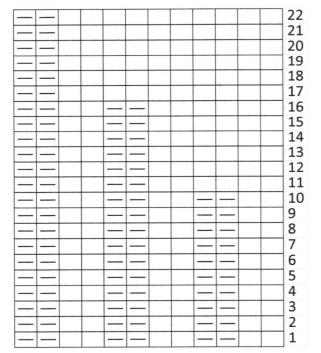

22
21
20
19
18
17
16
15
14
13
12
11
10
9
8
7
6
5
4
3
2
1

Work as set until mitten measures 3½ (4, 4½) in / 9 (10, 11.5) cm or 1 (1¼, 1½) in / 2.5 (3, 4) cm shorter than desired hand length.

Next rnd: [K16 (18, 20), pm] twice.

Dec Rnd: [Ssk, knit to 2 sts before m, k2tog] twice. 4 sts dec'd.
Knit 1 rnd.
Rep last 2 rnds once more, then work Dec Rnd 4 (5, 6) more times. 8 sts rem.

Cut yarn, thread through rem sts.

THUMB

With larger needles, place 9 (11, 13) sts held on waste yarn onto 2 dpns, join yarn, and pick up and knit 1 st from the base of the hand cast on. 10 (12, 14) sts.

Work in St st until thumb measures 1½ (1¾, 2) in / 4 (4.5, 5) cm from its base or desired length.

Dec Rnd: Work k2tog until 6 sts rem. Cut yarn, thread through rem sts.

FINISHING

Weave in all ends and block lightly following the ball band instructions.

	knit
—	purl

FOOT THINGS

BREAMISH

These classic socks are perfect in their simplicity. The pattern is worked from the cuff down with a short-row heel and a ribbed leg that both hugs the leg and helps the sock stay up in place.

SKILL LEVEL

Intermediate difficulty – Knit, purl, working in the round, simple increases and decreases.

SIZES

Finished foot circumference 5½ (6, 6½, 7, 7½) in / 14 (15, 16.5, 18, 19) cm. Shown in size 6 in. Designed to fit with minimal positive ease.

MATERIALS AND NOTIONS

1 skein of Spud & Chloë Fine (80% wool, 20% silk; 248 yds / 227m per 65g skein); #7818 Green Bean.

US #2 (2.75mm) set of dpns. Adjust needle size as needed to obtain correct gauge.

Stitch markers, yarn needle.

GAUGE

30 sts and 40 rnds = 4 in / 10 cm in St st.

PATTERN

CUFF

CO 40 (44, 48, 52, 56) sts, pm, and join to work in the round.

Set up rib: [K2, p2] around.
Work as set until Rib measures 3¼ (3½, 4, 4½, 5) in / 8.5 (9, 10, 11.5, 12.5) cm.

SHORT ROW HEEL

The heel is worked over half the leg sts.

Set-up Row: K20 (22, 24, 26, 28), pm.

Short Row 1 (RS): K19 (21, 23, 25, 27), w&t.
Short Row 2 (WS): P18 (20, 22, 24, 26), w&t.

Short Row 3: Knit to 1 st before the gap, w&t.
Short Row 4: Purl to 1 st before the gap, w&t.

Rep last 2 rows 4 (5, 6, 7, 8) more times. 8 sts rem unwrapped.

CLOSE SHORT ROWS

Short Row 5 (RS): Knit to wrapped st, work it tog with its wrap, w&t.
Short Row 6 (WS): Purl to wrapped st, work it together with its wrap, w&t.

Rep last 2 rows 5 (6, 7, 8, 9) more times. All sts will have been worked with their wraps. 40 (44, 48, 52, 56) sts.

FOOT

Resume working in the rnd and work even until foot measures 1 (1¼, 1½, 1¾, 2) in / 2.5 (3, 3.5, 4, 4.5) cm shorter than desired foot length.

TOE

Rnd 1: *K1, ssk, knit to 3 sts before next marker, k2tog, k1; rep from * once more. 2 sts dec'd.
Rnd 2: Knit.

Rep last 2 rnds 3 (4, 5, 6, 7) more times. 24 sts.
Work Rnd 1 twice more. 16 sts.

FINISHING

Place sole and instep sts onto parallel needles and graft together. Weave in all ends and block if desired following the ball band instructions.

COBBLES

With just a hint of nubby texture, the knit-and-purl stitch pattern in these socks is easy to follow, and the fabric of the leg grows fast on the needles. The angora/wool blend lends the fabric a plush feel and will felt slightly with wear, making these the perfect socks for a chilly morning walk.

SKILL LEVEL

Intermediate difficulty – Knit, purl, short rows and working in the round.

SIZES

Finished foot circumference 5¼ (6, 6¾, 7¼, 8) in / 13.5 (15, 17, 18.5, 20.5) cm. Shown in size 6¾ in. Designed to fit with minimal positive ease.

MATERIALS AND NOTIONS

2 skeins of Classic Elite Yarns Lush (50% angora, 50% wool; 124yds / 112m per 50g skein); #4490.

(This yarn has been discontinued. Good substitutes include Naturally Sensation and Adriafil Carezza.)

US #9 (5.5mm) set of dpns. Adjust needle size as needed to obtain correct gauge.

3 stitch markers, yarn needle.

GAUGE

24 sts and 32 rnds = 4 in / 10 cm in St st.

STITCH PATTERNS

INTERRUPTED RIB (MULT OF 2 STS)

Rnd 1: Knit.
Rnd 2: Purl.
Rnd 3: [Sl1, p1] around.
Rep Rnds 1–3 for pattern.

PATTERN

LEG

CO 32 (36, 40, 44, 48), pm, and join to work in the round.

Set up rib: [K2, p2] around.
Rep last rnd until piece measures ¾ in / 2cm.

Change to Interrupted rib pattern and work until piece measures 3 (3½, 4, 4½, 5) in / 7.5 (9, 10, 11.5, 12.5) cm.

HEEL FLAP

Heel flap is worked back and forth over the foll 16 (18, 20, 22, 24) sts, place rem sts on holder.

Row 1 (RS): [Sl1, k1] across.
Row 2: Sl1, purl to end of heel flap.

Rep Rows 1 & 2 until heel flap is approx square, ending with a WS row.

TURN HEEL

Row 1 (RS): Sl1, k8 (10, 12, 12, 14), ssk, k1, turn.
Row 2: Sl1, p3 (5, 7, 5, 7), p2tog, p1, turn.

Row 3: Sl1, knit to 1 st before gap, ssk to close gap, k1, turn.
Row 4: Sl1, purl to 1 st before gap, p2tog to close gap, p1, turn.

Rep Rows 3 & 4 until all sts have been worked. 10 (12, 14, 14, 16) sts rem.

Next rnd: K5 (6, 7, 7, 8), place EOR marker, k5 (6, 7, 7, 8), pick up and knit 1 st into each slipped st along side of heel flap, pm, knit across instep sts, pm, pick up and knit one st into each slipped st along the other side of heel flap, knit to end.

SHAPE GUSSET

Rnd 1: Knit to 2 sts before m, k2tog, knit to m, ssk, knit to end. 2 sts dec'd.
Rnd 2: Knit.

Rep Rnds 1 & 2 until 32 (36, 40, 44, 48) sts rem, 16 (18, 20, 22, 24) sts between markers.

Work in St st until foot is 1 (1¼, 1½, 1¾, 2) in / 2.5 (3, 4, 4.5, 5) cm shorter than the desired foot length.

TOE

Rnd 1: *Knit to 2 sts before m, k2tog, ssk; rep from * once more, knit to end. 4 sts dec'd.
Rnd 2: Knit.

Rep Rnds 1 & 2 another 2 (3, 4, 5, 6) times. 20 sts rem.
Rep Rnd 1 twice more. 12 sts rem.

FINISHING

Place sole and instep sts onto parallel needles and graft together.

Weave in ends and block if desired according to the ball band instructions.

PEGWHISTLE

Worked from the cuff down, this sock's rib pattern transitions into stockinette through the leg portion of the sock. Work these in an Aran-weight yarn for a quick, satisfying sock that even your kid cannot outgrow before they're ready for wear.

SKILL LEVEL

Intermediate difficulty – Knit, purl, working in the round, simple increases and decreases.

SIZES

Finished foot circumference 5¼ (6¼, 7, 8) in / 13.5 (16, 18, 20.5) cm. Shown in size 7 in. Designed to be worn with ½–1 in / 1.5–2.5 cm of positive ease.

MATERIALS AND NOTIONS

1 skein of Blue Moon Fiber Arts Gaea (100% merino wool; 305yds / 279m per 226g skein); Deep Unrelenting Gray.

US #8 (5mm) set of dpns. Adjust needle size as needed to obtain correct gauge.

Stitch markers, yarn needle.

GAUGE

18 sts and 27 rnds = 4 in / 10 cm in St st and 3×1 rib pattern slightly stretched.

PATTERN

LEFT LEG

CO 24 (28, 32, 36) sts, place EOR marker, and join to work in the round.

Set up pattern: [K1, p3] around.
Rep last rnd once more.

Next rnd: M1R, pm, ssk, work each stitch as it presents itself to end.

Next rnd: Knit to m, m1R, sm, ssk, work each stitch as it presents itself to end.
Rep last rnd until there are 4 sts between marker and EOR marker.

Next rnd: Knit to m, sm, k1, p3.
Rep last rnd until leg measures 4 (4½, 5, 6) in / 10 (11.5, 12.5, 15) cm from cast on.

Place last 12 (14, 16, 18) sts you have worked on holder, keeping markers in place.

RIGHT LEG

CO 24 (28, 32, 36) sts, place EOR marker, and join to work in the round.

Set up pattern: [P3, k1] around.
Rep last rnd once more.

Next rnd: Work each stitch as it presents itself to last 2 sts, k2tog, pm, m1L.

Next rnd: Work each stitch as it presents itself to 2 sts before m, k2tog, sm, m1L, knit to end.
Rep last rnd until there are 4 sts before marker.

Next rnd: P3, k1, sm, knit to end.
Rep last rnd until leg measures 4 (4½, 5, 6) in / 10 (11.5, 12.5, 15) cm from cast on.

Next rnd: Work in patt across 12 (14, 16, 18) sts and place them holder, keeping markers in place.

HEEL FLAP (BOTH SOCKS)

Heel flap is worked back and forth over next 12 (14, 16, 18) sts. Rem 12 (14, 16, 18) instep sts are held on holder until needed.

Row 1 (RS): [Sl1, k1] around.
Row 2: Sl1, purl to end.

Rep Rows 1 & 2 until heel flap is approx square.

TURN HEEL (BOTH SOCKS)

Row 1 (RS): Sl1, k6 (8, 8, 10), ssk, k1, turn.
Row 2: Sl1, p3 (5, 3, 5), p2tog, p1, turn.

Row 3: Sl1, knit to 1 st before gap, ssk, k1, turn.
Row 4: Sl1, purl to 1 st before gap, p2tog, p1, turn.

Rep Rows 3 & 4 until all sts have been worked. 8 (10, 10, 12) sts.

Next row (RS): K4 (5, 5, 6). Resume working in the rnd, and place new EOR marker here.

HEEL GUSSET (BOTH SOCKS)

Set up rnd: K4 (5, 5, 6), pick up and knit 1 st into each loop along the side of the heel flap, pm, work across 12 (14, 16, 18) instep sts, pm, pick up and knit 1 st into each loop along the other side of the heel flap, knit to end.

Rnd 1: Knit to 2 sts before m, k2tog, work to m, ssk, knit to end.
Rnd 2: Work each st as it presents itself.

Rep Rnds 1 & 2 until 12 (14, 16, 18) sole sts rem. 24 (28, 32, 36) foot sts.

Work even until foot measures 2 (2¼, 2½, 2¾) in / 5 (5.5, 6.5, 7) cm shorter than desired foot length.

LEFT FOOT

Next rnd: Knit to m, m1R, sm, ssk.
Rep last rnd twice more.

RIGHT FOOT

Next rnd: Knit to m, sm, work to 2 sts before m, k2tog, sm, m1L.
Rep last rnd twice more.

TOE (BOTH SOCKS)

Set-up Rnd: *K6 (7, 8, 9), pm; rep from * to end.

Dec rnd: *Knit to 2 sts before m, k2tog, sm; rep from * to end. 4 sts dec'd.
Next rnd: Knit.
Rep last 2 rnds until 4 sts rem.

FINISHING

Cut yarn and thread tail through rem sts to cinch.

Weave in all ends and block if desired following the ball band instructions.

CANNONFIRE

Worked from the cuff down with a simple colorwork pattern through the sock's leg and a band of colorwork around the toe.

SKILL LEVEL

Intermediate difficulty – Knit, purl, working in the round, colorwork, simple increases and decreases.

SIZES

Finished foot circumference 5½ (6, 6½, 7, 7¾) in / 14 (15, 16.5, 18, 19.5) cm. Shown in size 6 in. Designed to be worn with minimal positive ease.

MATERIALS AND NOTIONS

1 skein of each Cascade Yarns Heritage (75% superwash merino wool, 25% nylon; 437 yds / 400m per 100g skein); #5631 grey (MC) and #5662 red (CC).

US #2 (2.75mm) set of dpns. Adjust needle size as needed to obtain correct gauge.

Stitch markers, yarn needle.

GAUGE

36 sts and 40 rnds = 4 in / 10 cm in St st and in pattern.

STITCH PATTERN

Rnds 1–5: Work chart (below).
Rnd 6: Knit to end, take marker off, k3, pm.
Rnds 7–11: Work chart.
Rnd 12: Knit to last 3 sts, pm. Remove previous marker when you come to it.
Rep Rnds 1–12 for continuous pattern.

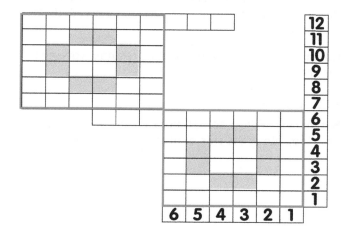

MC
CC

PATTERN

CUFF

With MC, CO 48 (52, 60, 64, 72) sts, pm, and join to work in the round. Distribute sts over 3 or 4 needles as preferred.

Set up rib: [K2, p2] around.
Work as set until Rib measures 1 in / 2.5 cm.

Next rnd: Knit and adjust the number of sts to 48 (54, 60, 66, 72).

LEG

Join CC and work in little o's pattern until leg measures 4 (5, 5½, 6, 6½) in / 10 (12.5, 14, 15, 16.5) cm from cast on, ending with Rnd 6 or 12 of the chart pattern. Cut CC.

HEEL FLAP

Heel flap is worked back and forth over next 24 (28, 30, 34, 36) sts. Place rem 24 (26, 30, 32, 36) instep sts on waste yarn until needed.

Row 1 (RS): [Sl1, k1] to end.
Row 2: Sl1, purl to end.
Rep Rows 1 & 2 until heel flap is approx square.

TURN HEEL

Row 1 (RS): Sl1, k14 (16, 16, 18, 20), ssk, k1, turn.
Row 2: Sl1, p7 (7, 5, 5, 7), p2tog, p1, turn.

Row 3: Sl1, knit to 1 st before gap, ssk, k1, turn.
Row 4: Sl1, purl to 1 st before gap, p2tog, p1, turn.
Rep Rows 3 & 4 until all sts have been worked. 16 (18, 18, 20, 22) sts.

Next row (RS): K8 (9, 9, 10, 11), pm. Resume working in the rnd.

HEEL GUSSET

Set up rnd: K8 (9, 9, 10, 11), pick up and knit 1 st into each loop along the side of the heel flap, pm, k24 (26, 30, 32, 36) instep sts, pm, pick up and knit 1 st into each loop along the other side of the heel flap, knit to end.

Rnd 1: Knit to 2 sts before m, k2tog, knit to m, ssk, knit to end.
Rnd 2: Knit.
Rep Rnds 1 & 2 until 24 (28, 30, 34, 36) sts sole sts rem. 48 (54, 60, 66, 72) foot sts.

Work even until foot measures 2 (2¼, 2½, 2¾, 3) in / 5 (5.5, 6.5, 7, 7.5) cm shorter than desired foot length.

Join CC and work Rows 1–5 of little o's pattern. Cut CC.

TOE

Sizes 6 & 7 only:
Set-up rnd: Knit to 3 sts before m, k2tog, k1, sm, knit to m, sm, k1, ssk, knit to end. 52 (64) sts.

All sizes:
Rnd 1: Knit.
Rnd 2: *Knit to 3 sts before marker, k2tog, k1, sm, k1, ssk; rep from * once more, knit to end. 4 sts dec'd.
Rep last 2 rnds 4 (5, 6, 7, 8) more times. 28 (28, 32, 32, 36) sts.

Work Rnd 1 four more times. 12 (12, 16, 16, 20) sts.

FINISHING

Graft rem sts together. Weave in all ends and block if desired following the ball band instructions.

ROAM SLIPPERS

Worked in chunky Montera, these slipper socks are perfect both for lounging around the house and for slipping inside wellies for extra warmth. The loose singles yarn felts well with wear, creating a soft but durable clog-like slipper. Knit these from the toe up with a short-row heel.

SKILL LEVEL

Intermediate difficulty – Knit, purl, short row heel and working in the round.

SIZES

Finished foot circumference 5¾ (6¾, 7½, 8½) in / 14.5 (17, 19, 21.5) cm. Shown in size 7½ in. Designed to be worn with approximately 1 in / 2.5 cm of positive ease.

MATERIALS AND NOTIONS

1 skein of Classic Elite Montera (50% llama, 50% wool; 127 yds / 116m per 100g skein); #3829 Aqua.

US #9 (5.5mm) set of dpns. Adjust needle size as needed to obtain correct gauge.

3 stitch markers; yarn needle.

GAUGE

18 sts and 23 rnds = 4 in / 10 cm in St st.

STITCH PATTERNS

Stockinette stitch: Knit every rnd when worked in the rnd. Knit 1 row, purl 1 row when worked flat.

PATTERN

TOE

With dpns, CO 5 sts, pm. Turn knitting and, working into the bottom of the cast on, pick up and knit 1 stitch into each cast-on loop with a second dpn, pm. 5 sts on each needle. As the stitch count increases, distribute sts over 3 or 4 needles if needed.

Rnd 1: [Kfb, knit to last 2 sts before m, kfb, k1] twice – 4 sts inc'd. 14 sts.
Rnd 2: Knit.
Rep previous 2 rnds 3 (4, 5, 6) more times. 26 (30, 34, 38) sts.

FOOT

Work in St st until piece measures 3 (3½, 4, 4½) in / 7.5 (9, 10, 11.5) cm shorter than desired foot length.

Separate work ready for heel: K3 (3, 4, 4), k7 (9, 9, 11) and place them on holder. 7 (9, 9, 11) sts on holder; 19 (21, 25, 27) sts on working needle.

Foot is worked back and forth from this point onward. Work in St st until piece measures 1¾ (2, 2, 2½) in / 4.5 (5, 5, 6.5) cm shorter than desired foot length, ending with WS row.

SHORT-ROW HEEL

Row 1 (RS): Knit to last 4 sts, w&t.
Row 2: Purl to last 4 sts, w&t.

Row 3: Knit to 1 st before wrap, w&t.
Row 4: Purl to 1 st before wrap, w&t.
Rep Rows 3 & 4 until 5 (5, 7, 7) sts rem unworked. 4 (5, 6, 7) wrapped sts on either side of heel.

CLOSE SHORT ROWS

Row 1: Knit to wrapped st, work st tog with its wrap, turn work.
Row 2: Purl to wrapped st, work st tog with its wrap, turn work.

Rep previous 2 rows 2 (3, 4, 5) times more.

Next row (RS): Knit to wrapped st, work st tog with its wrap, knit to end.

Next row (WS): Purl to wrapped st, work st tog with its wrap, purl to end.

CUFF

Set up rnd: Sl1, *p1, k1; rep from * over heel sts, pick up and knit 1 st into each loop along the side of the sole, pm, k7 (9, 9, 11) front sts, pm, pick up and knit 1 st into each loop along the other side of the sole.

Rnd 1: [K1, p1] to 2 sts before m, k2tog, knit to m, sm, ssk.

Rnd 2: [K1, p1] around.
Rep previous rnd twice more.

FINISHING

Weave in ends and block if desired according to the ball band instructions.

YARNS USED

The following yarns were used in this book. Many thanks to those companies who provided yarn support for this project.

Blue Moon Fiber Arts
bluemoonfiberarts.com

Blue Sky Alpacas
blueskyalpacas.com

Cascade Yarns
cascadeyarns.com

Classic Elite Yarns
classiceliteyarns.com

Debbie Bliss
Mirasol
designeryarns.uk.com [UK] / knittingfever.com [US]

Jil Eaton Minnowknits
minnowknits.com

Knit Picks
knitpicks.com

Lorna's Laces
lornaslaces.net

Malabrigo
malabrigoyarn.com

Madelinetosh
madelinetosh.com

Manos del Uruguay
artesanoyarns.co.uk [UK] / fairmountfibers.com [US]

Spud & Chloë
spudandchloe.com

ABBREVIATIONS

approx	approximately
beg	beginning
BO	bind off (cast off)
CC	contrast color
cdd	centered double decrease
cn	cable needle
CO	cast on
dec('d)	decrease / decreasing / decreased
dpn(s)	double pointed needle(s)
EOR	end of round
foll	following
inc('d)	increase / increasing / increased
k	knit
k2tog	knit 2 stitches together
kfb	knit into front and back of stitch
m	marker
m1L	make 1 left: insert left needle under horizontal strand between st just worked and next st from the front to the back, knit through the back loop
m1R	make 1 right: insert left needle under horizontal strand between st just worked and next st from the back to the front, knit through the front loop

m1RP	make one right purl: insert left needle under horizontal strand between st just worked and next st from back to front, purl through the front loop
MC	main color
p	purl
p2tog	purl 2 stitches together
patt(s)	pattern(s)
pfb	purl into front and back of stitch
pm	place marker
rem	remain(ing)
rep	repeat
RH	right-hand
RS	right side
rnd(s)	round(s)
sl	slip
sm	slip marker
ssk	slip 2 sts individually as if to knit, then knit those 2 stitches together through the back loops
st(s)	stitch(es)
St st	stockinette stitch (stocking stitch)
tbl	through the back loop
tog	together
w&t	wrap and turn (short rows)
WS	wrong side

ABOUT KATYA FRANKEL

© M. Waller

Katya Frankel is a knitwear designer and pattern writer. Her work has been featured in *Interweave Knits*, *Knit.wear*, *Knitscene Accessories*, Interweave's gifts and holidays issues, *The Knitter*, *Petite Purls*, *More Knitting in the Sun*, Unique Feet, and Artesano.

She lives in Newcastle upon Tyne, England.

ACKNOWLEDGMENTS

Many thanks to the people without whom this book wouldn't have happened:

Shannon Okey, my publisher, for thinking this book was a great idea and taking me on once again. Elizabeth Green Musselman, the editor and layout magician, who is such a pleasure to work with. I love what she's done with the book layout so much, and her ability to sense your writing style is awe-inspiring. Joeli Caparco, the tech editor, for making sure my patterns are error free, clear, and easy to follow.

My models – Anthony, Bridget, Joseph, Luke, Sophie, and Timothy – once again, you were superb to work with. Freya and Lloyd, for keeping me up to date with teen accessories trends. Miriam and Richard Waller for introducing me to the beautiful Bolam Lake and entertaining the children through what turned out to be an insanely long six-hour shoot.

And last but not least, my family: my husband, Daniel, and my children, Sophie and Timothy, for always being there for me.

katyafrankel.com

ABOUT COOPERATIVE PRESS

partners in publishing

MORE KNITTING FOR KIDS FROM COOPERATIVE PRESS

Boys' Knits
by Katya Frankel

Fresh Designs: Kids
ed. Shannon Okey

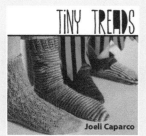

Tiny Treads
by Joeli Caparco

Cooperative Press (formerly anezka media) was founded in 2007 by Shannon Okey, a voracious reader as well as writer and editor, who had been doing freelance acquisitions work, introducing authors with projects she believed in to editors at various publishers.

Although working with traditional publishers can be very rewarding, there are some books that fly under their radar. They're too avant-garde, or the marketing department doesn't know how to sell them, or they don't think they'll sell 50,000 copies in a year.

5,000 or 50,000. Does the book matter to that 5,000? Then it should be published.

In 2009, Cooperative Press changed its named to reflect the relationships we have developed with authors working on books. We work together to put out the best quality books we can and share in the proceeds accordingly.

Thank you for supporting independent publishers and authors.

cooperativepress.com

CPSIA information can be obtained at www.ICGtesting.com
Printed in the USA
LVOW02s1053031213

363577LV00002B/6/P